BRIGHT LIGHTS & DIM BULBS

Bright Lights & Dim Bulbs

Jonathan Salem Baskin

iUniverse, Inc.
New York Bloomington

Bright Lights & Dim Bulbs

iUniverse books may be ordered through booksellers or by contacting:

iUniverse
1663 Liberty Drive
Bloomington, IN 47403
www.iuniverse.com
1-800-Authors (1-800-288-4677)

ISBN: 978-1-4401-7840-5 (sc)
ISBN: 978-1-4401-7841-2 (ebook)

Printed in the United States of America

iUniverse rev. date:10/13/09

Table of Contents

Introduction

2009 was one of the most insanely strange, creative, difficult, rewarding, and utterly entertaining years in recent memory.

If you're in the business of marketing, I can understand if you're not laughing about it, though. You're probably still in shock. Not much of it made much sense, and it didn't help that the running narrative in the mainstream media and blogosphere was obsessed with what was new, different... and, oh by the way, why aren't you with the program already?

On my blog, Dim Bulb, I kept asking one question all year long: *what program?*

Everybody had an answer, usually attached to a sales pitch. A case history to copy. The "five things you need to do" list to urgently follow. A wonderful metaphor, like *your brand is a promise*, or *social media is an ongoing conversation*, which usually meant you should spend money on it...even if it wasn't clear what "it" was.

I sometimes thought the folks who presumed to grasp what was going on were so caught up in the chaos that they really didn't have any perspective. Tactics often got called strategies in the adulation of headlines, or the brilliance of slide presentations.

So I went back and read a year's worth of essays. I reflected on what I'd written, with no sales pitch in mind, nor any preconceived notions about what topics would be the catchiest or easiest to talk about.

Surprisingly, I uncovered patterns that hadn't emerged during the year; themes that cut across many of the topics that we'd heard about, only in new and different ways. Every time I uncovered a new, underlying "it," I distilled conclusions that you can apply to your business, and then aggregated the relevant essays into the chapters in this book.

Then I went further, and created indices that reference essays by industry category and company name. You will find these tools at the end of the book.

Whether you're a dim bulber or first-time reader, my hope is that you will not only be entertained, but that you'll find uses for the essays and conclusions all year long. Read this book by chapter, look up companies in which you're interested, or thumb through to a few posts when a proposal, idea, or news event motivates you.

I suspect the future is going to be crazier and more challenging than the past, so here's to good reading, better business, and having a good laugh!

Jonathan Salem Baskin

Chapter One
Slogans & Gibberish

Who would have thought that 2009 would witness the continued resurgence of the written word?

The language was sometimes indeterminable, and the conversations often unrepeatable without a blush added to the shrug, but text has proven amazingly resilient as a communications medium. Words "work" on printed pages and mobile phone screens (i.e. cross-platform), find utility for marketing strategies old and new (you can use them to declare, or to converse), and prove convenient and adaptable for users young and old.

But if video killed the radio star, wasn't multimedia supposed to obliterate text?

2009 suggested otherwise. Text is a "hot medium," if you buy into Marshall McLuhan's theories about media (and I do, for the most part). Even when viewed online, words engage a single sense, and thereby establish a direct connection that is richer in specific information and meaning than more participatory, or "cool" multimedia experiences. When we're blown away by a video, we translate it into words to label our reactions, code our memories, and subsequently share our thoughts.

Yet, while text and words thrived, it was a banner year for slogans and gibberish in business communications, from nonsense adjectives in press releases, to incomprehensible statements about branding. Companies spent time orchestrating faux conversations instead of contributing to real ones; corporate strategies were described in incomprehensible doublespeak; popular phrases, like "innovation," were used to obfuscate the purposes of new management teams, as well as new products.

Why do businesses use words so poorly?

Maybe because words seem "free" when compared with the cost of producing a video or sound file. Perhaps because social media conversations are so fast and frequently that specific word choices seem less important. One of my pet peeves is that we still use words to satisfy ourselves; we talk to our aspirations for our brands, and not to make those "direct connections" to readers.

I think the year proved that what companies say *matters*, whether as the inputs into social media, or as the tool by which they make those direct connections with their consumers. But it has to be accurate, honest, and credible. It's harder to get away with a lie when it's literally spelled out; conversely, if we use words to state truths (and avoid all of the nuances that distract or lessen them), then text is a powerful tool that transports across technology platforms, and works with all age groups.

Here's what I gathered during the year on the importance of words, whether written or spoken:

1. Consider closely the necessity of every adjective in your next press release. Is your product really "world class," and what does that mean, anyway?

2. Markets, industry categories, and technology platforms are not people, nor do they possess interests or emotions as nouns in sentences. You're talking about what you do to other human beings so address them directly. Don't use buzzwords, like "innovation," as shorthand for something meaningful (spell it out instead) and, conversely, don't invent terms to cover-up the fact that you aren't saying anything meaningful.

3. Tell communities things that really matter, not just what your brand lexicon might dictate.

4. Review your mission and values statements, as terms like "customer-centric" or "market leadership" are kind of like saying that your company is going to exist, or that you think people should breathe air. Find ways to translate those goals into real, tangible ends that you can describe without coming across as generic.

5. Think action verbs instead of descriptive adjectives. Sentences that have nouns and verbs, and communicate some obvious action, are more compelling (and trustworthy) than phrases full of endless adjectival brilliance. Otherwise, nobody understands them, let alone believes what you're trying to say.

6. Words get connected to other words, one idea links to another, or news announcement to tangential fact, so you can't make declara-

tions in a vacuum. Anticipate these various contexts, and write for them.

7. Declarations don't obscure or override reality, they describe them. This means that your readers fact-check what you say, even if they do so unconsciously.

8. So you can't declare your way out of one reality, and into another. Words are "hot," so they mean something.

9. What you say should be preceded by what you do, not the other way around.

10. "Truth" isn't synonymous with "conversation" or "engagement." It's objective fact, not a strategy or process. Don't tell a story. *Tell a story clearly*. Finding ways to use words in real, compelling ways will be one of the key strategies for successful companies over the next few years.

Here are 10 essays to illustrate what I'm talking about:

(1) Copping a Better Slogan

The Minneapolis Police Department has painted its squad cars new colors, hatched new slogans and tag lines, and otherwise embraced a full serving of branding.

A firm called Kazoo Branding stepped up to the challenge of helping the force burnish its reputation within minority communities. It seems the cops have a history of brutality complaints, and suffered a racial-discrimination complaint by five high-ranking officers in 2007. The big idea was to recruit more minority officers.

So they went to a branding firm?

I mean no slight to the project, which selected absolutely beautiful colors for the squad cars. The new tag line – "Be looked up to" – is a fine statement, even if its English is a little strained. Kind of like "think different," right? The cops got a second slogan, too, which reads "To protect with courage, to serve with compassion." Posters for the campaign have a retro-happy-thing going, which I actually like.

But back to my question: why a branding firm?

The Chief of Police reports that the project has been a stunning success. "This year's recruiting class is 50% minority, the highest percentage in department history." Buried in all the blather about how the police rank-and-file thought the approach was utter hooey, there's the revelation that "a greater emphasis" put on placing ads and materials at schools, churches, job fairs, community centers, and other places where the force might connect with minority applicants."

Duh. They recruited more minority candidates by recruiting more candidates.

Nothing else changed, really. Whatever polices and procedures were however responsible for the alleged insensitivity to racial minority communities weren't part of the branding analysis. The character and conduct of the rank-and-file officers who'd earned the negative reputation by their actions (and/or by their omissions) didn't likely appear on the brand architecture, DNA, or whatever nonsense metaphor Kazoo used for expressing its findings. None of the soaring words of the new slogan had actions and metrics attached to them.

*It's a miracle of branding….*until reality catches up to it.

Let's give the Minneapolis Police the glossy new paint jobs and pretty posters. Fine. But wouldn't it have been far more meaningful if the force had instituted a study of the behaviors that had earned it the bad brand reputation, and then launched substantive changes in addition to the nice new visual branding?

Granted, the strategy could be to simply inject a mother load of minority officers into the force, and hope that they'll effect de facto change. But *that* wouldn't be a miracle of branding either, would it?

You can't cop a better slogan. You've got to live it.

(2) A Mercenary By Any Other Name

Blackwater Worldwide, the company of mercenaries responsible for shootouts in Iraqi traffic jams and general mayhem-for-hire around the world, has announced it is changing its brand name to "Xe."

Barely is branding used to make a business effectively disappear, but that's what's happening here. Blackwater is a manifestation of two current trends: outsourcing, and the privatization of government. It is to killing people what

IBM is to running IT departments; its policing and training capabilities much like an Indian call-center, or far-flung corporate supply chain. Our government annually paid it almost $500 million over the past few years, so that it could do a lot of the fighting and logistics work that used to get done by the U.S. armed forces.

The problem is that both trends are falling out of favor these days.

Outsourcing is one of those concepts that looks absolutely brilliant and obvious on paper (or in a glossy slide presentation), but often wrecks utter havoc when put into practice. Steps in a supply chain, not just the items or ingredients themselves, should get done wherever in the world the work can be best accomplished. The technology exists to virtually manage a distributed manufacturing process, whether assembling airplane parts, or artists creating a movie. A lot of marketing money (and the work-hours of thrilled journalists) has promoted the idea to execs looking for ways of looking smarter, while paying for the privilege.

So when an outsourced fastener maker misses a deadline for its step in assembling Boeing's new 787 airplanes, it doesn't just grind a factory floor to a halt, but rather throws businesses around the world into disarray. Lots of production schedules get whacked instead of one.

A six degrees of separation approach to manufacturing lets distant factories skimp or skip entirely on safety compliance, and deliver lead-painted toys to Mattel and other toy brands.

Anybody old or wise enough to remember the bad old days of making things would have known that the risk exposure inherent in outsourced manufacturing was possibly greater, or more dangerous, than even the best insurance policy might hope to mitigate.

In the instance of Blackwater, outsourcing gave the American people – its ultimate employers – contractor behavior in Iraq that wasn't always accountable to the rules our military are supposed to follow. Perhaps they were hired for that very quality, which is a frightening proposition in and of itself. Privatization of government services is another bugaboo for the Blackwater brand.

Another bugaboo is the premise that for-profit endeavors can do a better job of handling public responsibilities: it begs the question of to whom, or what, are they accountable? We all know that government is inefficient, bloated, and wasteful...but at least we know where their offices are located, and have some leverage to un-elect the leadership should we get too fed up.

Government processes are somewhat transparent, which is one of the reasons we know how screwed up they are.

Giving up that involvement in the name of better efficiencies means giving up some modicum of authority, doesn't it?

That's not to say that outsourcing can't work, or that there's something wrong with every privatization scheme, but the combination of the two trends – outsourcing government responsibilities, and not explaining them explicitly – puts Blackwater in a very difficult position, however high the profit potential might be in it. It's in risky businesses that we really don't want to hear about, or we're probably going to insist that our government not abrogate its responsibilities.

Hence the branding change...from a well-known and mostly disliked name, to something that is short, has no associations, and is impossible to pronounce. Xe was picked because it had "the best potential for brand identity," according to a company spokeswoman quoted in the *Wall Street Journal.*

Branding worded to make a brand invisible. Once out of sight, the potential for these modern-day Hessians is endless.

(3) Just Another Secret Code

The newly reformulated Powerade contains "ION4," and the branding emphasizes the secret code for this new concoction at the expense of the name of the product. I'm not sure that's such a smart thing to do.

The brand refresh actually makes a lot of sense. Gatorade invented the sports drink category in the mid-60s, and recently went through its own update, though of logo and not recipe. Powerade has always seemed like an also-ran, introduced a few decades later and commanding less than a fifth of Gatorade's market. So its product development decided to play to this circumstance of history, and claim a better, more current understanding of the hydration needs of the human body.

ION4 is "The Advanced Electrolyte System" that makes it work better and faster that Gatorade's 50 year-old science, or so Powerade's marketing would have us believe. Its strategy to label these ingredients, and feature it prominently in its labeling and advertising.

I think it obfuscates a potentially useful functional benefit with some outdated thinking about words and their meaning.

You've never heard of ION4 before. It's a made-up term, probably confirmed by Coca-Cola's crack legal team to connote no meaning or sense of ownership anywhere on the planet. So I can't imagine that anyone is comforted by its mention, let alone inspired by it, or terribly interested in taking the time to decipher what it might mean. It's not like a community of sports enthusiasts created it, or some loose affiliation of sports doctors have heralded its invention.

It's secret code, which is another dumb vestige of schmarty-pants branding.

Marketers filled the latter-part of the 20th Century with lots of nonsense claims and terms for product benefits: more *surfactants* in dishwashing liquid; greater *stain-removal power* in laundry detergent; added *somethingoranother* in gas. It still happens a lot today, as evidenced by Comcast's claims of *super-dooper* Internet speeds, or the nonsense propagated about digital music file formats. They're all secret codes that marketers presume to claim and then offer as unique benefits.

Only they're not benefits. I'd argue that consumers either don't have time for this nonsense, or they're empowered and motivated to see through it. ION4 requires more explanation; it's more work, not less. A hurdle, not shorthand.

Wouldn't it have been lots easier and more obvious to stick a "new" or "improved" starburst violator on everything? It's a tried-and-true tactic, only it's simpler, and it lets the brand keep visual space for, *er*, the brand name. All the creative talent that went to the elaborate web site to present ION4 could have been directed at making the *our-formulation-is-current-and-theirs-isn't positioning* more immediate and motivating.

Instead, we get just another secret code.

(4) A Tower of Babel

Macrovision changed its name and brand positioning last month, and is now to be known as Rovi Corporation. The CEO's press release explaining the move is a veritable Tower of Babel of ambiguity, confusion, and doublespeak, so it's a good case history example of what you don't want to say when you do the branding thing. Here's what he said, along with my interpretive thoughts along the way:

"Over the past two years, we have been focused on an ambitious strategy to change the digital entertainment experience."

Oh, OK. Thank goodness somebody was focused on changing it. I'm not sure what "it" is, or how any company that most consumers have never heard of had anything to do with it to begin with. But cool. This is obviously big stuff.

"As a result, we have made dramatic changes to our solutions portfolio."

Dramatic as in "who shot J.R.?" We like drama, and drama is certainly newsworthy. I just wish I knew what a "solutions portfolio" was. Is it a software thing, or some advisory service populated by crisis counselors? Maybe it's a collection of widgets, or a list of the answers to various geometry proofs?

"With our leading guide solutions and extensive entertainment metadata, we believe we are now positioned as a key enabler for digital entertainment."

Whoa. Lots of buzzwords there. Are these solutions different from the portfolio mentioned a moment ago? Metadata sounds like it's philosophy, or some heavenly tracking mechanism; the fact that it's extensive is good, isn't it? Was Macrovision not a "key enabler" for digital entertainment before the name change? It has been ambitiously changing it for two years already. I'm confused.

"Today's announcement is the next step in uniting our technology and people under one shared identity..."

So it has been changing everything with its people and technology *disunited*? Why bring them together now, and what does "together" mean? A shared brand name and logo on business cards doesn't really matter. Maybe there's some substantive structural change underway, although wouldn't it have merited a mention?

"...allowing us to move forward in creating a highly enjoyable entertainment experience for the consumer."

It's official: I have no idea what they're talking about. I couldn't tell you what the new company does, makes, or provides; I haven't a clue about the problems in digital entertainment it's trying to fix, or good things it wants to expand upon; and there's no explanation of why a change in branding has anything to do with anything that's yet to come down the pike.

Rovi's new brand sure says a lot while saying absolutely nothing.

(5) Writing the Sequel

Late last week, Procter & Gamble revealed its sales expectations for the next few years, and things don't look good: 2009 will increase 2 or 3% (below prior forecasts), and 2010 will be worse, perhaps climbing only a percentage point or two above flat.

I give P&G credit for even providing such guidance, as so many other companies have used the current economic malaise to throw up their hands and avoid it altogether (which I think is the same thing as admitting they have no idea what they're doing).

But the company is in a pickle: its profit margin on premium-priced household staples is threatened by a sharp decline in household spending, combined with an increase in the availability of just-as-good, but much cheaper brands. The competitive pressures are going to stick around, even when the economy improves.

Its plan? To lower prices and sell cheaper new products, while finding new qualities to add to its brands so that consumers will pay more for them, whether now or later on. "Innovation is P&G's lifeblood," said CEO Lafley to investors. "It stimulates growth in our industry even in economic downturns."

Squeeze me?

I know that P&G wrote the book on consumer packaged goods marketing. Legions of people trained in its crucible of brand management have gone on to teach generations of marketers how to lead brands as businesses, and never write plans that can't fit on a single page of paper.

The rub is that the book it wrote was conceived in a different time and place, and its theological truths aren't eternal, but rather deeply ingrained in the context and language of the 20th Century.

At its core, the P&G bible reads like this: first there was The Concept, followed with other ideas and feelings attached to it, which are then distributed to The Consumer. Chapter and verse declare reasons why people should pay more for whatever it was P&G sold, and consumers genuflected accordingly.

P&G has worked valiantly to keep its faith, doing everything from inviting every conceivable new media guru to reveal new doctrine in Cincinnati, to swapping employees with Google to better immerse itself in the future.

If there were any chance that it could adapt its time-tested ways to this new world of ours, P&G would have already done it. More importantly, it would be yielding sales and profit results. Only it isn't.

"Innovation" doesn't stimulate growth, other than in the bank accounts for all the consultants who wax poetic about it. It's just a word.

P&G's challenge isn't to find ways to make square pegs fit in round holes: *the key is to make round pegs*. Only that would mean changing the very words in its canon:

- People don't want to join a social network to talk about their toothpaste.

- They don't need to "engage" with brands, but rather need to clean clothes, etc.

- New media aren't channels as much as places.

- Every conceivable element of brand perception is now beholden to the reality of experience.

- The context of brands – from competitive choices, to the "noise" of the economy, and life in general – are integral aspects of branding, not apart or around it.

So no amount of defining "innovation" based on old ideas is going to cut it. I think we're talking about the needs for "complete reinvention," or "blowing everything up, and rebuilding it anew." A marginally better Tide laundry detergent won't command the price premium the company needs. Only a different one will.

This is the sort of heretical language in which the sequel to the consumer packaged goods bible will be written. As of last week's announcement, I don't think P&G has figured out that it needs to start thinking about writing a new book.

(6) And We Go Pre, Pre

The latest TV spot for Palm's Pre smartphone resurrects a song from the early 1980s, and uses it as background for some pale wisp of an actress to spout off Zen nonsense about traffic lights turning green.

It seems to build on an earlier spot featuring the same android-like androgynous woman surrounded by hundreds of monks in orange gowns dancing Busby Berkeley patterns as she chants about her life.

Though it's all quite atrocious, at least it's consistent.

The *Pre* deserves better. It has received pretty good reviews, and the folks at Palm have serious claims to owning a lot of the history and thought-leadership in the area of smart mobile devices. It also faces a ton of smart, well-financed competition from RIMS (Blackberry) and Apple's iPhone, so it risks being an also-ran, or just another gizmo that doesn't make consumers' consideration lists.

The challenge is to carve out a unique position, or purpose, for the *Pre*. Find a thing or activity that it uniquely enables or supports. Risk being explicit on a functional benefit (or list thereof, if the phone is a good as I think it is). Help consumers finish the sentence "I should consider a Pre because..."

The branding campaign for the Pre doesn't even come close to meeting that challenge.

I'm all forgiving new life to the song *Doot Doot*, from the West German band Freur. I would have never connected it to a smartphone; it's this ethereal, kinda sad dirge that always gave me an existential German *oh-this-is-so-horribly-beautiful* vibe. The band was famous for about a nanosecond before returning to the ether. They deserved better, just like the Pre.

The campaign confuses tone with content, and this presumption that we can use words and images to connect disparate emotions to things – instead of consumers doing the connecting through their experience – leads lots of otherwise smart marketers down the wrong path. It would have been a lot stronger had the creative been based not on making some abstract point, but rather telling us something explicitly memorable.

Then, the Pre branding gurus could have gone out and found a song to use. Maybe something with the chorus "better management of contacts," or "I found the website faster." Hell, AT&T paid Oasis millions to write a song from scratch for its commercials a few years ago (oops...but it said nothing, and you only heard two beats of it).

(7) The Digital Shakedown

Ever seen a slide filled with colorful logos and wacky names, purportedly portraying the crowded, utter confusion of the world of social media? Sometimes it's shown with another slide, most often a graph showing a line for consumer time spent with traditional media (trending down), and a line for "engagement" with things online (going upwards).

My bet is that you've seen these slides in a presentation from a digital agency or new media expert, during which you were told to do two things:

- Be scared, and throw out every sensible expectation you ever had for marketing, and
- Just do it, and buy some of that social media stuff.

The sales closer probably included a few examples, or "case histories," of companies just like yours that did the same thing you're about to do...i.e. got the same presentation, freaked out, and spent money on social media campaigns. They did it because others had done it, and now it's your turn. Whatever you accomplish will be used to get the next client to succumb.

Sound familiar? Next time one of these conversations approaches, I'd like to suggest another reaction:

Refuse the Digital Shakedown.

There's no reason you have to do social media, or that you're somehow an idiot Luddite because you aren't spending lots of money on digital stuff. There are infinitely important ideas to explore in social spaces – from product development and enterprise-wide performance management, to the changes in the ways consumers find, learn, adopt, and promote products and services – but you'll never even touch any of that if you're getting sold a digital marketing campaign from people who sell digital marketing campaigns for a living. It's like expecting to explore the vagaries of architectural history and lifestyle behavioral theory with a real estate broker. No slight intended to either salesperson, but their ulterior motives tend to discount the agnosticism of their views.

So here are three suggestions for what you might want to tell them next time you're subjected to one of those presentations:

1. Flip the telescope, and look at what your company is trying to accomplish, not start with what the social space offers. If someone showed you an issue of, say, *Town & Country*, and told you that you had to educate and reconfigure your entire company so it could be represented in the magazine, you'd laugh them out of the room, right? Come up with some clear business goals first (and "getting into the social space" doesn't count).

2. Define the objectives in behaviors, not engagement (or some other made-up metric). The rest of the company isn't looking for you to redefine marketing; they want you to discover new ways to deliver the

actions that matter to the business. For every activity that you need to ask for more patience than usual, or squishier metrics that make the old measures for branding seem like an exact science, the more likely you've lost touch with this reality. And you'll risk your job once your associates figure out that your cheaper marketing spend didn't produce anything close to actual sales.

3. Keep looking for negatives, not searching for positives. There's ample material claiming the benefits of social media. We all think it's cool, and it certainly does have loads of promise. *Check*. Now try to talk yourself out of doing it. Ask the presenters to poke holes. What's missing? What doesn't connect, or doesn't completely make sense? Get somebody outside of marketing involved in the conversation, both for perspective, and to keep you sober.

"Hey, everybody's doing it" is a rationale that convinced our weaker-constituted friends to start smoking in grade school. Fear of being left out, and of being wrong, is powerful incentive to take action. Don't let yourself get bullied, or dazzled by busy slides. Ask tough questions at the next presentation.

Resist the Digital Shakedown.

(8) Manufacturing Truth

The *Scientist* magazine reported last week that pharma giant Merck had invented its own peer review medical journal in order to better hype its products; of 29 articles, almost two-thirds referred to Fosamax or Vioxx.

And we're surprised?

Medical journals go to doctors as a reliable source for continuing education. Peer review is how scientific discoveries and applications are vetted, and then embraced or rejected. So faking it, even if said source contained legitimate information but otherwise excluded other, potentially contradictory stuff, stops just shy of outright falsehood. *Almost.*

The magazine in question sure looked legit, even if the ads only hyped Merck products. An editorial board was conscripted, although it doesn't seem that they actually did anything except get a paycheck I think they charged money for the thing, just to add a daub of verisimilitude.

We communicators have been doing this kind of thing for a long time.

Back in the early days of my career (think *Mad Men*, only with shaggier hair), it was standard practice to organize faux public-interest groups, associations, or committees to help hype whatever our clients wanted to sell. We'd dummy up letterhead, list an address (usually our agency office), get a phone number, and start plastering the cosmos with purportedly objective insights.

This proud tradition hearkens to Ed Bernays' founding of a group to promote greasy bacon as part of a "healthy breakfast" just past the start of the 20th Century. Some would say the practice goes back much further, to the Vikings use of it when they got disinterested ship captains to tell would-be immigrants that a barren, frozen, far-away island was "Greenland."

Now, it's lots easier to do. The Internet means that anybody can pose as an expert on anything – a number of digerati advocates will claim that possessing an opinion literally makes someone so – and post/share what might seem like legitimate information. That's why there are sites that give detailed, otherwise-believable support for even the most insane subjects. Atlantean aliens. Global conspiracies. The Information Age has given way to the Age of Chaos, as there's no standard, reliable way online to discern fact from fiction. I wonder how many kids show up at school with reports citing web sites that "prove" the Holocaust didn't happen, or that the Apollo 11 landing was faked on a Hollywood soundstage?

So this Merck nonsense is no surprise. But it's still kinda scary, for a few reasons:

- We're talking about medicine. Any pharma company (or any company at all) has the right to publish its own propaganda, but the stealth nature of this program suggests that Merck was trying to deceive people. So go ahead a lie about whether your brand of golf balls really fly farther than another, but twisting the facts on whether prescription drugs work or not is, well, frightening.

- We're talking about doctors and administrators. If these people can sell-out to the highest corporate bidder, how can we believe anything that they tell us? You think that your tap water is safe? Now, that web site that explains how fluoride is a plot to control your mind starts seeming a little more reasonable?

- We're talking about a medical publisher. The ersatz Merck publication didn't come from a smart ad agency, but rather a division of Elsevier, which publishes the real ones, too! How are we supposed to trust anything it produces?

The bigger issue, however, is that "truth" has become a commodity that anyone can manufacture, whether by a corporate flack in an office, or a lone nutcase typing in his mom's basement. Merck got caught, but thousands of similar offenses pass into our accepted versions of reality every single day.

(9) Unlimited Supply (EMI)

In an industry that is either all about the money, or all about the art, I don't think it's surprising that Guy Hands and his fellow buyout gurus have failed to find a sustainable middle-ground with EMI Group Ltd.

The expert financier bought the storied label of Beatles fame for a few billion in 2007, and proceeded to stage The Full Buyout Dance:

- Massive infestation of management gurus.
- Ruthless slashing of budgets.
- Imperious implementation of scientific processes.
- Endless & purposeless ideation sessions, and
- All of the other words and actions of the well-honed *acquire-and-flip* approach to business.

Only it's all about the art, which is available in all but unlimited supplies, and in any number of different configurations. EMI is at risk of trying to collect tolls on a canal or road that has no traffic. No amount of managerial brilliance, or expert buzzword phrasing, can change this fact.

Hands' minions are rumored to be building robust Internet content to promote the label's artists, but the fundamental fact is that EMI is in the business of selling square pegs in a marketplace that seems willing to reward only round holes.

And then it's all about the money.

It's a popular myth, this idea of the business guru parachuting into an ailing industry and proceeding to tell wizened old execs how to zip-up their own flies. Books have been written about it (and them), and the business press perpetuates the fantasy. Everything has a "recipe," and the titans of industry are like great cooks.

The reality is never that easy or fun; in the case of the music industry, a vast number of highly intelligent, creative, capable people are already struggling to come up with a way to make money. So far, they've failed miserably, for the most part. The likelihood that Hands ever had "the answer" were slim for starters, and his accomplishments so far – offending artists, or driving them away outright, for instance – suggest even less of a chance he'll get it right, no matter how brilliantly he describes his brilliance.

All he had to do was look a bit beyond his celebrated brain trust (or perhaps value more the talent inside EMI?), and he could have seen that the future of music, as well as digital content of any sort, is being invented all over the world: subscription models replacing packaged-goods distribution; participatory experience, like the video games *Guitar Hero* and *Rock Band*; democratized production, which forces down costs and thus makes profits easier (albeit smaller); multi, or transmedia development, so the very idea of one medium being discreet from another goes the way of the dodo bird.

EMI is busy trying to put its corporate finger in the hole in the dike through which music is streaming. That must have been an extra-credit class at B-school.

(10) What Will Citi Stop Doing?

Citi's announcement that it'll fire 52,000 people begs a basic question: what will it do to its brand?

No, I don't mean the impact of the bad news. Every business other than Wal-Mart and your local pawnshop seems to be in trouble these days, so we're talking tears in rain here (thank you, Roy Batty). I doubt that anybody will switch their checking account because their emotional attachment to Citi has been damaged by the bad news.

However, there may well be customer defections based on what Citi has chosen to stop doing. That's 52,000 (and 17,000 already dismissed this year) less people to do the account transfers, count the cash, or do whatever else banking industry personnel are supposed to do. Approximately 1/10th fewer people will work for Citi when this blood-letting is over.

So what will it do differently?

I mean, that's the real question about the brand, isn't it? Its experts can label the moves however they choose, and I bet there's more than one glossy, highly creative ad campaign somewhere in its near future. The nonsense they've been running this year can only run so far before somebody looks up and notices that Citi's brand has very little to do with what it says about itself (or fantasizes about its customers in a Joe the Plumber sort of lifestyle marketing way). Their answer will be to run different nonsense, I'm sure.

So the real impacts on the company's brand won't come from the marketing department. Customer relationships with Citi will change. 2,000 fewer employees mean 104,000 fewer hands to answer phones, click computer buttons, or whatever. I wonder what new fees will get charged, or services reconfigured to be "customer-directed" (a great code word for "outsourcing work to your clients")?

What services or insights will simply disappear entirely? I read that the company will "jettison some companies that aren't core to its strategy," whatever that strategy might be...but the rest, well, for all we know, the company is going to try to keep on doing the same things it does now. Only with far fewer people.

However it plays out, it'll be these activities – or the lack thereof – that'll impact its brand far more than any narrative coming out of its communications department, or from its agencies. It's these changes that will define Citi's branding going forward, and not its Wall Street valuation (its stock price tanked today), nor its ranking on any branding agency favorites list.

If it were really forward-looking, Citi would define and express these changes, and make them the substance of its outbound marketing. Explicitly tell people what'll change, so they're not disappointed or surprised. Promise them the good things that'll happen, presuming there are any.

We wonder why corporations rank so low on matters of authenticity and trustworthiness. I think it has something to do with making utterly incomprehensible announcements (and business decisions) like this one. We customers aren't totally dim bulbs, are we? We know that a company can't fire a tenth of its work force and continue on with business as usual.

Things will change, and they most likely won't be good for us. But Citi isn't telling us what, who, or when. I suspect we'll get to discover those answers on our own. And in doing so, we'll define the Citi brand.

Just For Fun: Shakespeare Did It

Supreme Court Justice John Paul Stevens has rendered a verdict: William Shakespeare couldn't have written the plays attributed to his pen. The likely author was Edward de Vere, the 17th Earl of Oxford.

This says lots about the nature of truth in the chaos of our Information Age...or the changed definition of how we make decisions in our Age of Chaos.

If there's one thing we know is true more than (and above) any other idea, it's that nothing is as it seems. Our capacity to digitally change visual and auditory records of history renders them as no more than creative expressions; the little places, points, and edges where we once had to look for evidence of manipulation – such as the staging of an event, the confirmation of a signature, or the obvious cut-out of a person or object in a photo – are now often proof of authenticity, as real things are often less perfect than manipulated ones.

The Internet has done the same thing to text, and to the content it expresses. No fact exists without a qualification or refutation, and the mechanism of online interaction elevates every viewpoint to simulacra of truth. Internet search, and the need for reporters and bloggers to present "another side" to every conceivable story or fact, means that nothing is as it seems, no matter how obvious or sacrosanct it might be.

Jesus was married. HIV doesn't cause AIDS, and inoculations are bad for you. The World Trade Towers were felled by dynamite blasts. Humans cavorted with dinosaurs on a planet Earth only 6,000 years old. The Rolling Stones' Brian Jones was murdered. President Obama will raise your taxes.

And Shakespeare didn't write his plays.

I mean, come on now, this is nuts, even if it's all good fun. How do we know that Socrates really said what Plato attributed to him? Where's the proof that it was FDR sitting at his fireside chats, and not an imposter? Since nobody was in the room with Einstein, where's the confirmation that he wrote his famous equations? Could Mozart's pen have been guided by someone else's hand?

Justice Stevens' case rests on all the circumstantial context stuff of a case before a court: the Bard didn't own enough books to explain the breadth of his knowledge; his education was wanting; he dedicated a few plays to somebody in the earl's family; the guy just wrote too many brilliant plays too quickly, and left little in the way of letters or drafts to attest to his struggles.

Welcome to *the Facebookification of history.*

Even in light of immediate, incontrovertible evidence, the perception of truth is still a perception. It's a conscious decision. Fact is, ultimately, *belief,* in that you have to trust that something is trustworthy. Truth is *a decision,* rendered in the "courts" of individual minds and hearts, and dependent on circumstance.

Our Age of Chaos blows up that decision-making process, though, or at least diffuses it, so there's no ultimate finding. Or it just extends the conversations endlessly. Nothing is set. Everything is changing, or questionable.

And we marketers think we can associate qualities with the toothpaste and car polish brands we sell? If the Shakespeare brand can't survive intact, I shudder at the prospects for Apple, or Bud.

Chapter Two
Almost A Great Idea

We usually try to mimic great successes, but I think there's more to learn from ideas that were just shy of wonderful.

2009 was full of really smart, strategic programs that were well conceived and delivered...and then stopped short of realizing their full potential. Usually, really good branding and marketing campaigns hit walls that were self-imposed, arising from limits of vision and expectation: when all you hope to do is influence awareness, measured when you choose to measure it, or intention (same thing, only squishier), you neglect to pursue additional avenues to realize broader business goals.

Ultimately, *action is what matters*, not the potential for it, and there were many examples of good ideas that didn't look beyond traditional marketing channels, or habits, to deliver truly great results, like:

- Viral videos that got watched a lot, but stopped short of prompting a sale (or getting consumers tangibly and reliably closer to one).

- Promotional campaigns that seemed too good to be true (promise overload that defied belief).

- A customer service problem that was adequately fixed, but not extended into a sale opportunity.

I also suspect that a lot of the year's best ideas went unnoticed because we're not trained to look for them in places outside of marketing's normal haunts. *Distribution*, for instance, was again proven to be a massively smart strategy to build a brand. *Finance* was another one. 2009 saw these activities going on either in parallel, or sometimes apparently unrelated to a notable marketing strategy. I was surprised to come across more than a few Dim Bulb essays that captured these points.

I could also pretty much bet that you won't get pitched any of the year's almost-great ideas or, if you're at an agency or consultancy, propose them to a client. It's fascinating to explore what happened, why it happened the way it did, and how it might have been improved even further. Perhaps some of the best strategies for you to borrow next time will emerge from the programs that were just shy of great last time?

The last year showed that two qualities differentiated "good" ideas from "great" ones:

- Operationalizing program elements beyond the traditional channels marketers use (so applying activities to areas like service, or finance).

- Asking for the sale. Probably the most notable shortcoming of really good programs was that they didn't risk being more bold in the sales close.

Here's what I found from analyzing a lot of almost-great ideas:

1. Try to strip out everything that 'worked' in a case history, so you can chew on what didn't. Getting insight into how those variables could have changed is probably far more useful (and reliable) than hoping to decipher the good news, and then trying to duplicate it.

2. Consider the possibility that more messaging isn't necessarily better messaging. I wonder if some nearly marvelous campaigns were impeded by including simply too much content?

3. The next element for a great campaign often comes from an unlikely source, whether inside or outside your company. The challenge and opportunity for your brand is not to apply it consistently across communications media (the easy question), but rather to operationalize it across the business (the harder one).

4. If something seems to work, contemplate what could be wrong with it. Sometimes, good programs operated very efficiently, but left opportunities untouched because nobody thought to look for more.

5. You might want to automatically discard the top cases of great successes that will emerge from various reviews of 2009. If quantum physics has any truth to it, you simply can't recreate these cases, by definition.

6. If you sell a product, you may achieve greatness by considering your offering as a service, and visa versa. I think that purposeful mash-ups yielded some of the year's most intriguing opportunities.

7. Be aware of your limits of vision, especially when it comes to engaging with your consumers. You're not in the business of entertaining

people, unless you're in the entertainment business. I was struck by how many companies wasted a lot of time and money trying to be funny, instead of using humor and other entertainment techniques to tell consumers stuff they really needed and wanted to hear.

8. Be deferential to preconceived notions; there's a context within which your consumers perceive your marketing (or overall business efforts), and there are also somewhat consistent attributes that apply generally to how people interpret information. Number thresholds are one such quality, as folks "get" the value of something priced just below an even number, but have trouble grasping the magnitude of difference between 100 and 150.

9. Invite non-marketers to every marketing and branding meeting. They'll provide a good grounding in reality, at a minimum, and hopefully yield new applications and ideas for your campaigns.

10. Ask for the sale. Again, the consistent difference between almost great and great programs was that the latter had the guts (and honesty) to ask for a sale, or at least a specific action. "Visit our web site" didn't count. *Sales* emerged this year as the most important metric, just like in every year prior.

Here are 10 essays that explore some of the great ideas hidden in really good ones:

(11) So Close, And Yet So Far

JCPenney went to great lengths to produce a funny video to promote its jewelry offering, and then failed to connect it to anything resembling a sales transaction.

It's branding, of course. So getting lots of people to watch, forward, or interact with it is benefit enough. I can't wait until it tries to tell that to the shareholders; November's comp store sales were down 11% from last year. Investors should be thrilled to learn that the company, and its agency Saatchi & Saatchi, chose to focus on increasing brand equity instead of making money.

That's not to say that *Beware of the Doghouse* isn't funny. The set-up is that a husband gives wife a vacuum cleaner for their anniversary, and gets banished to a doghouse that hides a subterranean prison for fellow romance-violated louses. The closing caption reads "brought to you by The Jewelry Store inside JCPenney," and is underscored with links to nominate someone to get stuck in the doghouse (submit a photo), forward to movie and, oh yeah, click on the store link.

I felt robbed after watching it.

The movie is funny, but only up to a point; then it gets really, really long (almost five minutes' worth of a joke that should have taken all of one). Worse, the concept is so smugly happy with itself that it forgets entirely to provide any relevance to this holiday shopping season. The campaign was promoted with the usual Twitter/Facebook nonsense that passes for community these days, so the entire shebang is intended to get people to have fun with the doghouse conceit.

Shouldn't it have tried to sell some merchandise? I'm not talking a hard sell, or anything as unpleasant as promoting a price (gasp!). There are lots of creative, funny ways to get would-be consumers closer to something other than adoration for branding creative. Here are five:

1. Where's the jewelry widget, in which you could enter various personality attributes for your loved one, and it would spit out possible gifts (and deals)?

2. How about a fembot IM app that you could talk to about your gal-pal? The helpful android could suggest gifts that were tied to buy now discounts, making the transaction (from branding to buying) real-time?

3. Maybe offer an online club for guys who've been in the doghouse, in which they could earn discounts or points toward purchase for doing things like advising one another, letting guest women grill them, or whatever?

4. How about a ranking tool that categorized various doghouse-destined "violations," and converted them into the appropriate jewelry gifts? Perhaps certain mistakes are so sever that it would take *two* distinct jewelry moments to rise back to the light of day?

5. Why not let visitors take out doghouse insurance, which would be some nominal purchase that gave the buyer quick access to a small set of jewelry options, pre-packaged to get shipped overnight to remedy a conflict?

Where were such better connections to the reality of behavior and purchase? Just because the video is intended to accomplish branding, I don't quite understand why it couldn't also accomplish selling. What good is the former if the latter doesn't sustain it? It's as if the video got to close to being relevant to behavioral reality, but then the marketers chose to stay away.

The brand experts relegated selling to the doghouse.

(12) I Didn't Know the Rules

I think the intimate relationship players have with videogames makes engagement with a brand seem like a bad blind date, but in both cases you've got to know the rules.

Last week, I flew Southwest. My dim memory of its open-seating policy got me to the airport at least 90 minutes before my scheduled departure, confident that I'd be the first guy to get on the plane. I was shocked when my boarding card put me about 120th. It seemed like every other passenger had got there before me.

I only learned later that you can check-in online within 24 hours of your departure, thereby receiving virtually your place in line. I was aware of online check-in, but had never used it for any other airline (why would I want to print my boarding pass at home when I can do it at the airport in about 20 seconds?).

Games are no fun when you don't know the rules. Neither are brands. I'm not sure there is, or should be, a difference between the two. We marketers want our consumers to:

- Understand the point of our product or service.
- Grasp the basics of using it.
- Feel a sense of inclusion and empowerment there from.
- Get rewarded for continued (or more frequent) use.

In fact, I'd argue that most of our relationships with the stuff we buy are games, whether or not we (or the brands) think that way. I get the rules for flying American; there are little user/player tricks that I know because of my repeat visits; I accrue status because of my successful, er, spending. Similarly, I was thrilled years ago to learn that ordering my hamburger "Animal" at In-N-Out Burger meant that it came fully loaded (*uh oh*, now I'm going to be killed for sharing that tidbit). I know the day/time of day that gets me the quickest appointment at my Honda dealership, and how to use the FAQ at my various technology sites of choice in order to fix problems that other customer/

victims have encountered. My wife shops Gap only when the prices have been marked-down to red-line goodness.

They're all games, and learning to play them means we feel more rewarded by them. And it means that it stinks when your ignorance of the rules means you can't enjoy the experience.

Southwest's sign-in policy shouldn't be a value-add trick for repeat users, as being unaware of it means that newbies have a distinctly bad experience. Any videogame designer would tell you that' it's why games have loads of up-front training (I'm convinced that you could vastly improve your brand value if gamer designed your customer training/service function).

So why didn't some box pop up immediately after I bought my Southwest ticket, telling me that I should remember to check-in online? Where were the suggestions from other seasoned travelers on what I should or shouldn't do? Couldn't the airline embrace this interface – home page as portal to a game – as a starting point for developing those engaging player relationships (instead of outsourcing it to third-parties)?

Don't get me wrong: Southwest does a zillion things right. But it did its best to make me feel like an outsider last week. And that makes me less likely to return to playing the game. *Oops*. I mean buying the brand.

(13) Why Stop At Gas?

Hyundai continues to innovate ways to differentiate and deliver its brand; its latest effort is an offer to guarantee a year's worth of gas locked-in at $1.49/gallon.

The idea, while a copy of something similar Chrysler tried last year, comes on the heels of its promise to buy cards back from buyers if they lose their jobs. Oh, and it happens to be building high-quality, rather stylin' cars, too.

This is brilliant branding, because it addresses the real needs of potential buyers, and doesn't twiddle with their fantasies or presumed penchant for social media blather. It extends Hyundai's marketing beyond the narrow confines in which most automakers compete (because within which their agencies are most comfortable). Creating a fuel program (or any other operationally-originating effort) could be far more meaningful branding than any amount of UGC about the brand.

It's a communications challenge, too, in that we consumers are a suspicious lot, and there has to be a catch that'll allow Hyundai to make more money than it deserves, right? Sure enough, its guarantee to pay for gas costs above $1.49 includes a mouseprint revelation that it won't refund the difference if gas prices come in below that threshold.

That's the nature of a hedge: one party shifts risk to another, thereby limiting its downside exposure by letting another entity assume the potential for some upside gain. Farmers have been doing it for a long time, as a guarantee of a needed profit on a crop still months away from harvest can be well worth giving up the potential of an even better return. Many commodities, including oil and currencies, are similarly traded via the mechanism of futures contracts.

Broadly speaking, "hedging" is what Hyundai has been doing for its customers since the economic meltdown began. Taking risk out of the car-buying equation. Brilliant stuff, in my book.

So why stop there?

Forget the car business and gas for a minute, and think about all of the other risks in our daily lives. Grocery bills. Docked pay for being late. Airline fares. Electric or heating charges. There are any number of expenditures that are held captive to the vicissitudes of market pricing. That variability represents some opportunity for benefit (playing the reservation game just right can yield better ticket prices), but are far more often the cause of unpleasant, costly surprises.

Imagine if you could hedge your weekly grocery bill? How about locking-in the cost of your most frequent air travel routes? Our new economy frowns on profligate spending, and uncertainty means this month's payment could become next month's burden. So why doesn't your local utility let you go beyond estimating your winter heating bill, and commit to an amount that worked for you...while letting a speculator who underwrote it buy the opportunity to profit if prices go down further that you'd thought?

Is this a growth opportunity for Pricelock, the company behind Hyundai's gas hedge? What about the insurance companies? Don't they assess risk for a living?

(14) Closer

As branding's flu season is in full swing, lots of companies are betting that getting people to transmit content is the same thing as making them interested in buying a product or service. Few of these flights of viral fantasy amount to anything more than a virtual sneeze.

Some are better than others, though. Sephora's "Mistletoe Makeover" comes closer to actually selling something. The idea is simple: upload a picture of a face, click on inconsequential Photoshop*ish* outlines of eyes and mouth, and then see the image rendered with sort-of full clown makeup (or is it Victorian prostitute?) and put on top of a dancing puppet character. Add a short message and then email the "surprise" to a friend or world leader.

A few neat tricks happen along the way. After dolling up your image, the various products used to *harlotitize* your face drop down as props on the screen; click on them, and you go to the store page. You can also choose to buy the entire combination of stuff you used. And, when you're done, you get a set of lashes or a mini-lipstick as a free gift with any purchase.

My bet is that some sales or operational folks had their say in developing this campaign, more than likely to the chagrin of the branding experts. God forbid anybody did anything with such viral nonsense other than pass it on; even the hint of relevance of purchase was probably a *tisk-tisk* capitulation to that irritating brand externality called the real world. The uneasy sales/marketing accommodation was an accomplishment, no question, but imagine if it had gone further:

- Consumers could go wild with the makeup. If the thing is truly supposed to be fun, why limit it to applying a combo that can't look real (the finished pics make faces resemble cadavers, though maybe that's just me)? Why not let people go nuts applying various items, perhaps incentivizing their behavior with greater discounts for more use (drop-in offers as they play) and/or forwarding? The pretense that the resulting images are supposed to look good is inane, however much on brand it purports to be.

- Let people give discounts to friends. Wouldn't it be nice if consumers could send discounts to one another (there's an implicit endorsement in that)? Why not let it be product-specific, perhaps linked to the campaign artwork? Prices are going to get slashed in-store about 5 minutes ago, so go ahead and link the discounts to something vaguely resembling a branded interaction.

- Have a life/continuation after the holidays. This idea that the only time people want to send stupid, useless viral stuff to one another ends the day after Christmas is at best mistaken, and at worst self-destructive. Shouldn't any communication be the start (or continuation) of an ongoing relationship with consumers? I have no idea what the creative should be for another dip into the viral vault in, say, February, but I bet there are more than a few possibilities.

Once the holidays are over, there's going to be lots of publicity about the traffic and forwards prompted by various viral campaigns. I'm sure we'll hear all about the dancing elves, for instance.

The important question to ask will be: how did they directly influence and/or support sales? If the answer is either "it wasn't supposed to," or perhaps simply a *shrug*, you might want to ask the question of a different vendor when contemplating your next campaign. Getting closer to sales impact is a good idea in a bad economy. Well, in *any* economy.

Maybe we're talking some branding makeovers in 2010?

(15) Zune Doesn't Fix Its Brand

As if on cue...well, actually very much according to the click of the clock...Microsoft's Zune players went dark on New Year's Eve. It was a missed opportunity to build the brand.

It had to do with the 30-gigabyte devices getting confused with leap year (or something), yielding an error message instead of a favorite song. The fix, dutifully noted via a header buried low on Zune's web site, read "Zune 30 FAQ: Trouble with your Zune 30? The fix is simple," was actually simple. That is, once you let the battery drain and then plugged your gizmo into your computer long after January 1, 2009 was well underway.

I don't mean to slight Microsoft for the glitch. It's easy to complain about the company, and I'm happy to do it fairly often, but technical snafus are a part of technical devices. Stuff breaks down or otherwise disappoints in every product category. What merits mention, I think, is how Microsoft responded to the problem. They fixed it, instead of approaching it as an opportunity to build the brand.

Zune users are a devoted lot, I'm told...all 14 of them, or however small the small segment might be. Microsoft has blown through millions trying to grow that base, but its marketing is usually more notable for its inane efforts to mimic the *iPod*. It literally can't buy awareness that is relevant and cool. So why didn't they go to town with their very own "Y2K for Zunes" moment?

- How about giving away "free minutes" to all current users?
- Quickly organizing a "2009-certified" sale at retail?
- How about a social media campaign to ask people what song they wishes they'd loaded on New Year's Eve, or what they would do if given an "extra day?"
- Or how about something wild?

Approaching the problem like a technical issue that needed to be fixed was evident of Microsoft's larger problem: where are its marketers when they're not busy trying to copy the competition's marketing?

(16) Fix My Face. Really.

Clarins Group, a French cosmetics brand, is rolling out spas in upscale department stores across the U.S., in an effort to provide facials as a catalyst for selling its products.

It makes sense from the perspective of the brand, of course: upscale cosmetics belong in spas, and are further credentialed by experts wearing white coats, wielding makeup brushes and handfuls of goop. The brand strategy is also intended to target Hispanic women, so I'm sure sometimes the spa experience will be conducted in Spanish. *Voila.* Brand experience equals product sales.

Not so much.

Spa visits are optional, and your average consumer considers them a luxury. Last time I checked, luxury choices weren't faring so well in this melted economy of ours. There's a cadre of consumers who visit department store counters for a close approximation of an entertaining experience (getting eyes done, etc.), but Clarins can't be planning on converting them, can it?

There's a much bigger opportunity here, and it has to do with thinking about brand as behavior, not image. Clarins should think less upscale spa, and more downscale Starbucks outlet. Skip offering luxuries or other options relevant to the brand, but rather find the routines that address consumer needs, and prompt ongoing behaviors. Here are a few nutty ideas:

- Morning Prep: Why couldn't women be offered a start-of-the-day treatment – sun block in the summer, moisturizer in the winter – priced at something shy of a cup of coffee, and taking all of a minute to apply? Make it a daily stop, offering subscription pricing and frequency discounts/benefits.

- Mid-day Refresh: What about the lunchtime refresher experience... something all of 5 minutes long, but including a face wash and some makeup application? Heck, why not make a take-away salad or sandwich part of the deal? Throw in a hair wash and dry?

- Evening Treatment: Take the mid-day deal and spice it up, letting women schedule customized visits prior to going out in the evening. Personal preferences could be stored, and a quick stop could let people prepare for a night on the town? There could be coordinated selling opportunities with other departments in the store.

Here's another wacky idea: *offer the same deals to men.*

The spa concept is generically inert; other than whatever presumptions the marketers possess about the brand, there's nothing unique or motivating about the offer. Cosmetics counters at department stores are mostly the engagement marketing corollary of a drive-by shooting.

But if Clarins focused its brand understand out to the routines and needs of its would-be customers, it might open up an entirely new approach to these time-worn ideas.

Don't offer merely to enhance my appearance. Fix my face. Really.

(17) AMC Gets With The Programs

Cable station AMC has announced a new slogan – "Story matters here" – and plans to market new original programming and themed movie nights. I'm intrigued by the idea that the station could give itself an identity, of sorts, perhaps in the spirit (if not the exact execution) of a Disney and its kid movies.

It makes sense as a branding strategy, especially when you consider the wash of cable programming, and how tough it is to make money in the content distribution business. Endless choice has made content effectively worthless, as you can pretty much watch anything, any time. I can find reruns when I want to find them, whether on my TV, or on a cable station. Some distributors, like HBO, SyFy, and Showtime (and AMC) have embraced exclusive, custom series as a way to engage and differentiate with viewers, but it's an expensive and potentially dicey strategy: for all the fans won over by HBO's *Sopranos*, I suspect an equal number were disgusted, and never again tuned in. Comedy Central has built its reputation on bold, original stuff that self-selects its customers.

So for most stations, producing new content could be seen as swapping the problems of the distribution business for the curse of the creative business, right? You can't please everybody all of the time, yet you've got to take risks when you're selecting what to put through the pipe that you own. What's the right balance?

AMC plans to mitigate this conundrum (well, after making it worse, as it has promised to air a remake of *The Prisoner*, which is a deep-dive into TV obscurity that will sure to deliver all of 12 viewers, myself included) by organizing "themed movie nights." This got me to thinking about how it could really make its content, and the resulting marketing, really unique and valuable, without risking narrowcasting to an ever-smaller audience:

- Lead with the movies: AMC was originally called "American Movie Classics," wasn't it? In a world wherein content is endless and thus pretty cheap, the need is for new authority and credibility; organizing and broadcasting movies by theme is a nice start, but it's nowhere near what it could be. Why not dedicate creativity and budget to developing programs for, around, and because of the movies? Dare to be insightful and/or funny, so produce a "*Godfather* Flicks for Beginners" program, followed with a "Spaghetti Westerns as Post-WWII Italian Narrative" show. Add value to the reruns and re-establish AMC as the movie channel...with more.

- Engage community on it: People care about movies, so what a great excuse to get people talking! Why couldn't AMC be the place where actors respond to viewer tweets while their work gets aired (or the conversation is somehow time-shifted)? Couldn't experts "host" conversations...think *Mystery Science Theater 3000* meets those sonorous actor interviews you can catch now and then on PBS? Think less movie nights that are basically scheduling exercises, and more events that drive viewer interactivity.

- Develop original programming based on community involvement: Sure, it's cool if you chance upon a *Mad Men*, but you still risk leaving lots of your viewers behind. Why not become the first cable network to crowdsource research on original content? Think of it as UGC-flavored development, and find ways to involve the AMC viewer community in choosing program topics, themes, and/ or even enlisting them in envisioning characters and plot lines. Why not invent mechanisms for enlisting their commitment to viewing programs (or buying merchandise schwag, or whatever) before putting the program(s) into development, and then involving them via a variety of tools during the creative process (video blog on creation, various polls to help get feedback on character or plot ideas)?

The branding slogan "Story matters here" is rich with possibilities, most of which need to be realized via programming and scheduling. AMC doesn't have to (and perhaps can't) try to pick and choose which stories matter, as much as find creative ways to institutionalize the activities, and then involve its viewers in the processes.

Hey, doing that might make for an interesting story!

(18) Not So Innocent

Coca-Cola intends to buy between 10 and 20% of Innocent, which is the company that all but invented the idea of a "socially conscious, good-for-you fruit smoothie" in the UK. I think it's a deviously brilliant move, but not for the reasons feted in the marketing media.

You'll read a lot about Innocent's branding brilliance...its unconventional marketing is considered *ethical* because it gives away lots of money, and maintains a cuddly, *we're-not-really-in-business-to-sell-stuff-to-you* tone in its ads, on its web site, and even on its product labels. This is why it has been successful, and now Coke wants to own a piece of it, and perhaps import some of those wise ways back to the Mother Ship in Atlanta.

I've got an alternate history for you to consider:

- Innocent concocts really fresh, simple, good-tasting drinks that it can legitimately claim are good for you.

- It introduces it to the market not through some creative brand marketing, but rather by *giving it away* to pretty much anybody who will reach for it with an open hand.

- It builds a reputation on this quality and directness, much like Apple has built its brand on the realities of its products and services.

- Competitive marketing departments *totally misinterpret* these truths – flipping the proverbial cart before the horse – and introduce at least a dozen copy-cat branding strategies in the UK. Now, there are lots and lots of smoothie products that come across as equally cute, cuddly, and at least somewhat ethical.

- Therefore, Innocent can't *own* a position, to use a typical branding term, or hope to command consumer preference based on its communications, which have mostly become *commoditized* (just as most words and images can be similarly generic).

What it *can* own is...wait for it...*shelf space!*

Forget trying to be the best, most cuddly brand communicator; I'd argue that one of Innocent's core growth/survival strategies is to be the *only* or *most visible* smoothie on store shelves. Think of how many more units it can move by being a part of a Coke products distribution scheme?

I'd call it a smart branding strategy.

I wrote about the idea that distribution is a branding effort far more important than much of the imagery that passes for it – the channeling of choice, really, versus what amounts to hoping for it – in some detail in my book, *Branding Only Works on Cattle*. Coke has actually written the book on this approach, really: for all the blather about *choice* when it comes to colas, where can consumers actually pick one over the other (past the grocery store shelves, where the cola companies don't make any money anyway)? Coke's success (and Pepsi's, along with the others' failures) is determined by exclusive or dominant distribution footprint, whether at restaurant fountains or sports stadiums.

So the Coke investment makes great sense for Innocent, and the UK smoothie's success will benefit Coca-Cola. It has everything to do with really smart business...and nothing to do with branding, charity, or anything so innocent.

(19) Too Good To Be True

You've probably seen TV commercials for magicJack, which promises free phone calls via a *gizzinta* for your computer's USB port. It's a VoIP deal, much like the telephony that your local cable offers you in one or more of its bundles, only magicJack's novel approach:

- Lets you use your regular phone.
- Embeds its software in the USB *gizzinta* (hence the "jack" of its magic)
- Never gets into any explanation of Internet packet transmission or how it works.

It's a phone service, sans any real customer service, so don't bother wondering anything more about it. Media reports say the company has sold a few million units, which means some serious coin. You'd think that its value proposition, if not the brand position, is unassailable. Mainstream competitors charge every month what magicJack costs for an entire year, not to mention additional set-up and/or service fees that magicJack apparently defers. Other Internet services, most notably Skype, still come across as very techie, in spite of the cuddly look-and-feel of the user interface, and the pricing models are somewhat complicated. And old-fashioned land-lines can't compete whatsoever on price.

So I say that it has a gigantic problem. *The offer is too good to be true.*

No brand exists in a vacuum; branding is delivered, and perceived, in an ever-changing context of the *Here-and-now.* It's one thing to present consumers with a clear, relevant differentiation, but when the difference is so glaringly, cosmically huge, it makes comparison not only difficult, but oddly irrelevant. It dares us to choose not just a better option, but wholly unique offer that literally defies comparison. It raises as many questions as it purports to answer, and I'd suggest it erects barriers to entry that otherwise wouldn't have been there. Sometimes sales message can just be *too good.*

It doesn't help that the commercials and web site look like they're repurposed from Pocket Fisherman and ThighMaster campaigns. Phone service is something that actually matters to a lot to people; that's why it was once considered a utility, like electricity and water. So it's hard to consider relying upon a provider that could just as well be selling countertop ovens. And it's kind of weird that there's no information about the company, nor any way to contact them (and the exploitation of the inventor's daughter and her cute puppies is shameless, to say the least).

And that's when I figured out the deal: it's not a phone service, and they have no intention of signing up users for Year 2 or beyond.

Customer service is the marketing program opportunity with VoIP, as the moving parts of PC hardware and software uniqueness, combined with the variability at numerous points in home or business Internet connections, means that problems are all but guaranteed. That's why Skype hasn't ever really taken off, and why many people reject the idea of letting their cable TV providers treat their phone problems with the same irritating disinterest. The magicJack deal might work fine right out of the box, or it might not. And it might not work the same a day, week, month, or year from now. For the price you paid, you get a *gizzinta*, and a promise.

Sure, some people will buy that sort of thing, but I wonder if it's a sustainable business. Maybe the marketing is wholly accurate: the offer is no different than one of those miracle vegetable choppers.

It's too good to be true.

(20) You Had Me At 100

Chevy worked overtime to produce a lot of buzz for the estimated 230 miles/gallon for its Volt EREV, and I'm not sure anybody cared. It wasn't as auspicious coming out party for the "new" GM. Too bad, because the Volt EREV (for Extended-Range Electric Vehicle) deserves the attention...and GM should get the credit. From what I can tell, though, they botched the announcement in at least three ways:

1. Picking a dumb number. What does 230 mean to anyone? It's not a common or obvious threshold, and it's so many times greater than the mileage anybody would expect for a car to be practically incomprehensible. Turns out no car has ever broken 100, so why not start there (nice round number that definitely feels like more than, say, 35), then throw in a couple dozen more for kicks? Since the EPA hasn't certified the MPG number yet, is there a chance that it could be lower than 230? The number almost begs to be qualified or made real-*er*, like by examining how many trees will be felled to produce electricity, etc.

2. Promoting it poorly. Ads of a "2" and "3" followed by a smiley-face electrical socket appeared on TV, along with the numbers "8-11." It was supposed to go viral and start a conversation. GM paid for all the requisite social media nonsense (Facebook page, YouTube videos, etc.), only there was nothing to talk about except the marketing itself. Imagine if the campaign had asked a question, like "where would you go if your car got 100 MPG?" or "why can't the rest of the world build a car that goes as far as ours does?" Declare something that explicitly asks for an answer (ergo, start a conversation).

3. Failing to encourage real participation. So the car is coming out sometime in 2010 and will cost a rumored $40,000. You think a lot of people are lining up to buy it? GM wouldn't know, because its social media campaigns have no real participatory purpose. Why couldn't it have used the announcement to start taking names, offering glimpses of the manufacturing process, and scheduling test drives? How about addressing the financing issue, and introducing

a plan now that would allow consumers to accrue some savings or discount benefit to then use when the car is for sale? Link it to the environment, or changing commuting habits (if I recycle so-and-so, I save X on the Volt, for instance). Give people real things to do, not just the fantasy nonsense of *friending* on Facebook.

The biggest disappointment for me is three-tiered, in that as a consumer, American, and a marketer, I cannot fathom why GM is failing to tell me a story about where the company is going. I understand that it got lots of money from the government, and that some ads promised "a new day," or whatever, but there's no obvious direction, narrative flow, or milestones to give its announcements any context or credibility.

Maybe nothing has really changed? Whether heavy metal tail fins or 230 MPG EREVs, it's all about pushing new models to dealers, and letting them haggle prices. Ford isn't doing much better, in that it announced last week that it was somehow linking up with electric utilities for electric cars. What a cool basis for a new, interactive, meaningful relationship with its customers, but it instead chooses to host stupid vlogs for its Fiesta launch.

What a bummer. I was ready to believe otherwise. And GM could have had me at 100.

Just For Fun: The Cosmic Significance of Flatulence

The journal *Science* last week reported that large plumes of methane gas had been detected on Mars, suggesting the possibility of geological or biological activity that are often associated with the presence of life.

Finally, flatulence gets its good name back as an indicator of good things.

Living things produce approximately 90 percent of all the methane gas on Earth. It's a chemical sign that transformative biological processes have occurred, usually involving digestion. The Mars researchers believe they've sensed seasonal differences in methane levels, which is reminiscent of the variation in the gas we might see here between, say, before and after a big dinner.

So is it possible that the key indicator of what would be the most incredible discovery in all of human history...*is a giant fart?*

Finding things based on their antecedents, by-products, or aftermath is a pretty standard scientific approach. Since all physical actions have reactions, it means everything that is observable is somehow, someway, sometime causally related to everything else. Equations are the literal maps of such interactions; theories are the models that propose the linkages. And then observation and measurement are the litmus tests that differentiate fact from really neat and/or hilarious propositions.

You can probably see where I'm going with this one: why can't we similarly lower ourselves to the same base level of physical truth when we look for evidence of brands?

No qualitative survey or focus group can claim causal relevance for branding to purchase decisions; there's no linkage that can be measured, only a connection inferred, suggested, or implied. Same goes for the outbound branding prior to purchases. We can try to measure, whether via conversation or fMRI sensing devices, what aspects of brands somehow register – for the moment we choose to sense them – but these mental states remain outside the purview of any direct connection to buying.

We can't write equations for brands, because the steps aren't linked by anything more substantive than dotted lines in slide presentations, or by the aspirational hopes of our employers and clients.

Instead of basing our branding equations on the demonstrable reality of who, what, where, when, and why people buy things from us, we chose to measure the vague merits of brand intention, presence, engagement, promises, or whatever.

That's just not the same as measuring, say, the levels of methane gas in the Martian atmosphere, because there are only two ways it got there. And you don't need a glossy metaphor to describe or understand them.

So where's the gas in the marketing world? I fear that it's mostly generated by all the experts who still have no real idea what they're talking about.

Chapter Three
Social Media's Promise

All the incessant chanting of new media's Greek chorus notwithstanding, 2009 revealed two emergent facts about the promise of social media: first, it's not really "social," and second, "media" is its least important quality.

The opportunities arise from what goes into it, and what comes out of it. Those are the dangers, too.

There was no shortage of experimentation during the year, and I wrote a lot about the thriving cabal of researchers, pundits, bloggers, and consultants who conspired to sell the idea of new media to marketers who were either disillusioned with traditional media (those pesky consumers just aren't doing what they're supposed to do!), or simply didn't have the budget to pay for it anymore.

It occurred to me that social campaigns cost less because they were worth less – i.e. the market pricing model works – and that it didn't make sense to replace the already-questionable metrics developed to support a few generations of branding and marketing with new ones that seemed even more vague. Yet we saw lots of really creative, memorable campaigns that captured clicks, downloads, and headlines...but not necessarily sales, unless you chose to hold up two events and suggest they were linked because they were concurrent.

If the metric for success is that things need to happen at the same time, we should credit social media campaigns with making the sun rise, and ensuring that gravity functioned correctly. Maybe we should put world peace on the docket for 2010?

Social media must promise more, and it does. There's an amazing amount of truly revolutionary thinking going on, but you have to look past the immediate examples of glitzy campaigns. It's impossible to understand the utility of social media campaigns unless you explore what goes into it – corporate behavior is much more important than creative marketing – and what comes out of it in terms of participant behavior (involvement yielding actions in the real world). It's just stunning to me that nobody's been keeping score: some of the most noted campaigns promoted brands by promoting conversations about the brand promotion.

What the year showed me was that it was less important to spend money on the mechanism of how these inputs and outputs are connected – the "social media" tools, whether Twitter, Facebook, or A Player To Be Named Later – and more crucial that businesses understand the connectivity at both "ends." Lots of companies figured out how to waste their consumers' time. The challenge for 2010 will be to discover how to earn it.

Here are my conclusions culled from a year's worth of coverage:

1. You don't have to do it, because there's no "it" to do. Social media are a vast array of approaches to connecting people. Understanding what you want to do is far more important than doing something, even though no services vendor will tell you that.

2. You're already doing it anyway. That's the funny quality of this medium; your employees, vendors, customers, and critics are chatting and shooting videos inside your offices, factories, or stores. Perhaps the biggest (if not first) strategic challenge is to understand the way things already are, before hiring a firm to launch a campaign. I don't think social media is about engaging with your brand. Your brand is an idea, like "patriotism" or "happiness." Consumers talk about marketing when they're given only marketing to talk about. Consider providing more meaningful information for them to engage with.

3. If you're chasing customer complaints on Twitter feeds, you're missing the bigger point: fix your customer service. For every tweet you get to answer, I guarantee that some multiple of customers have silently abandoned your business. Ditto goes for bad chat room posts. Address the underlying situation (i.e. inputs) instead of trying to manipulate the conversation.

4. Social media chatter isn't the same thing as brand preference (whatever that is), and it certainly doesn't mean you've accomplished anything lasting. Your latest Facebook campaign might have a beginning and an end, but social media interaction is ongoing, and real-time. Are you measuring this? More importantly, *why* are you measuring it? How much of this conversation is nothing new/not terribly important?

5. Be very critical of any argument for social media that requires you to reject "old fashioned" ideas of sales conversation. People have been

talking since the days of ancient Sumer, and marketing's challenge has *always* been to convert this natural phenomenon into tangible business benefits.

6. Don't start a blog: they're a burden, and nobody is asking for you to do it (except your friendly digital marketing firm). Don't start videotaping yourself for distribution on YouTube. Your audience hasn't asked for a conversation with you about anything. Figure out what they really care about, and what's the really best way to share that information with them?

7. Today's social media PR crisis is tomorrow's distant past; flash mobs are a permanent fixture compared to the tempest of chat room or tweets (as evidence by the quick rise and fall of attention to Iran's election in 2009).

8. Think before you react, if you react at all.

9. If all you can think of giving to your customers is some marketing artifact (ad mash-up or purposefully inane web video), hold off until you can discover a more important purpose. Again, don't confuse noise with actual conscious attention.

10. Consider what comes after conversation. It's not likely an immediate sale, so where are your programs that accomplish something other than entertaining your customers?

Here are 10 essays to further your internal conversation about social media:

(21) A Grain of Salt

The *Wall Street Journal* dedicated a special section in yesterday's paper to "The Secrets of Marketing in a Web 2.0 World," and made five shockingly novel revelations:

- Don't just talk at consumers.
- Give them a reason to participate.
- Listen to and join conversation outside your site.
- Resist the temptation to sell, sell, sell.
- Don't control, let it go.

I know, I know, it's hard to catch your breath after reading such insight! It took a partnership with MIT's *Sloan Management Review*, and the expert thinking of academics from around the country to reach these (and similarly earth-shattering) conclusions.

In other words, it's hard work getting things so completely wrong.

Marketing experts, whether academic or self-proclaimed, can't resist issuing rules, laws, or predictions, especially this time of year. It often represents the exact opposite of what everybody else should believe or do, usually due to a combination of factors:

- They wear rose-colored glasses. There's an *a priori* assumption that marketing is all about mental states, and it affects everything said experts think. It also means that they're only looking for branding evidence in communications media.

- They have a sales agenda. Whether driving kids into classrooms, or clients into contracts, it's hard to have an objective conversation about any phenomenon if the thinking is controlled by people who make money on 1) said phenomenon, and 2) controlling it.

- They're also confused. Qualitative measures of branding are the proverbial tip of the iceberg to all the behavioral underpinnings of such awareness; like hammer-owners, the experts only see the nails. When marketing experts are busy sending tweets at one another every nanosecond, it's hard for them to imagine, let alone see, a vastly larger world wherein that's not necessarily what people choose to do.

Yet it's these very people who presume to lecture the rest of us at industry events and conferences. And we can look at the sales collapse this holiday season – or the plunge in corporate reputation, dissolution of trust in brands, and the evaporation of premium pricing – and still listen to this stuff without laughing? Here are the real secrets:

- Don't just talk at consumers, do things. Behaviors are the drivers of awareness, intention, referral, or any other quality we ascribe to mental states about brands.

- Give them a reason to participate, but not to simply participate in/ with your branding. People don't want to talk about ads, or turn the web into a glorified suggestion box. 2.0 activities don't describe marketing, they are the marketing itself.

- Forget blanket participation in conversation, and how about instead starting with making the stuff you write on your sites more honest and direct?

- Absolutely sell, sell, sell. Everything you produce should have utility, relevance, value, and meaning for your target consumers; if this isn't the textbook definition of selling, then it should be. Are we really supposed to expect to distract consumers into purchase?

- Keep control of your authenticity. You should actually try very hard to control the conversation, in that your relationship with would-be consumers should have some overarching direction, flow, and context. You can't guarantee everything will fit it, but "letting go" is only exciting to people who have no responsibility for what happens next.

Good luck with the other lists (there are lots of them out there already). My advice is to take them all with a grain of salt, if that.

(22) The Twits at Motrin

I'm a dim bulb, but I think that it's fun to watch a miraculous event coalesce into religious canon. Motrin just added a parable to the Social Media Holy Book.

The marketers behind the popular pain killer ginned up an online ad about moms and the back pain that comes from carrying babies in shoulder pouches, or slings. It wasn't particularly original or funny, and it had zero utility content (i.e. it didn't tell would-be consumers anything usefully new). In other words, it was pure branding, and it seems the goal was to get people talking about it online.

It's via such conversation that marketers are supposed to reach consumers, now that it's been deemed politically-incorrect to actively (and honestly) try to sell them something. Converse they did. Well, more like rant, one after another, in a process that my friend Alexander Wolfe at *InformationWeek* calls "versation." The primary engine was Twitter, a service whose 140-character message limit seems intended to keep people from sharing anything substantive. However, these tweets – I think the notes should be called twits – are perfect for expressing either pointless or blunt emotions, like boredom, or anger.

Thousands of messages declared that the campaign was offensive, more than a few calling for a boycott to protest Motrin's trivialization of women's pain and a favorite baby-carrying technique. A day later, the campaign was pulled, and apologies were issued from a clearly chastised corporate spokesperson. So prepare to get lectured on what Motrin did running any new marketing. Create more forums for them to use, and spend more time and money getting their approval. And, whatever you do, do more of it next time, because there are always more and newer technologies and services that let people connect.: there's always a self-anointed, often anonymous collection of people who constitute an "influential audience" you should talk to prior to doing whatever you planned to do

I'd like to offer up a slightly different, perhaps apocryphal epistle for any marketer about to receive the accepted wisdom of Motrin's parable: *It's about your branding, stupid.*

If you choose to market pointless, irrelevant things, chances are there's at least one community somewhere, online or off, that will hate you for it. A far larger percentage of consumers will simply like and trust you less. The idea that any marketing strategy would get invented exclusively to use social media is itself just plain dumb; you'd never invent a unique reason to run billboards, or hire people to walk the streets wearing placards, would you?

There's no reason that you *have* to use *any* media, unless your brand strategy calls for it. Trying to guesstimate what people will think is funny or cool is a losing proposition, with a downside far greater and more likely than any upside. So trying to earn recognition for it, let alone hope that it'll somehow, someday translate into purchase-influencing memories is, well, kind of like throwing dice in craps: it's not branding, it's gambling.

And if you think that there's some inherent value to just doing it (or your CEO does because of that latest story in a business magazine), you should plan for any and all reactions. I guarantee you that somewhere there's an expert who believes that Motrin's campaign was an utter success because it got people talking. Full stop. Give them something to do other than complain.

I think that social media programs need a purpose other than buzz or conversation. It's just too easy for it to become a vehicle for sharing anger or a complaint. You need to envision motivations for doing good things (could there have been some collective vow to buy J&J products because of something it did?). The fact that in this example the network was buzzing about an ad, and not about things that might matter – like ethical sourcing, employee benefits, career advancement for women, actually moderating pain – tells me that the complainers were less influenced by broad principle than they were irritated by immediate circumstance.

But coming up with a behavior you want to get out of a social media program is a good litmus test of whether or not you should get into one. Like

I said, we're going to see the Motrin story added to the theology of social media. Get prepared for the sermon at your next marketing conference, or hearing about it in the next agency pitch. Everyone is going to try to teach us things about it.

I just wonder if there's really anything there to learn.

(23) Friends With An Airline

Late last month, American Airlines launched a social media campaign to register 10,000 New York area "friends" on Facebook. I think the program evidenced a number of neat ideas, though ultimately revealed the limitations of social media as currently defined.

First, the smart stuff: the campaign was goal-oriented, in that the 10,000 participant target made the request real. People like to be a part of something with a purpose, even if it's nothing more than a numeric abstraction. A goal also means that something has a beginning and an end, so it seems more authentic, and participating feels more immediate.

Second, it promised a payoff. The pitch was easy to understand, and compelling: friend AA, and get your friends to do the same, and you'll get access to some special promotions once the participation target is reached. While not exactly an explicit *quid pro quo*, it did give the friending behavior a sense of purpose.

Third, the first two points provided the context in which qualitative content about AA, its routes, services, and related passenger experiences could be posted. This allowed the airline to encourage de facto evangelism without asking for it directly; there's nothing better than such organic storytelling.

OK, so what's wrong with all that?

Technically, nothing. It's great delivery, and an actionable list of 10,000 people who've opted-in to a sales promotion distribution list is a great accomplishment for AA (for a cost of, what, something close to nothing)?

It's just not friendship. Nor is it a relationship with the brand, or an active, functioning community in any sense of the term. When American's VP of Sales comments "...what better way to create a tighter bond with our followers than to ask them to join us on Facebook," he's either kidding, or just stupid. There's no bond here; it's a nice promotional idea, and that's about it.

American Airlines already has its true loyal mechanism, and it's called a frequent flier program. As such, it's woefully underused. Bob Crandall's genius was to create a metric for fliers to grasp and monetize their relationship with the airline. Frequent fliers are already much more than friends of the airline, and it makes the idea of Facebook "friends" almost laughable.

So far, this promo further proves that Facebook is a glorified distribution list. AA should use it, and Twitter, and any other social media technology *du jour* as actively and intelligently as it can. This campaign shows that it knows how to translate said programs into meaningful returns for its business.

But it's not friendship, nor is it community, is it?

(24) Then So Should a Car Wreck

If the eyeballs delivered by the viral nonsense coming from Burger King is considered marketing, then so should a car wreck.

Various campaigns that riff on the Whopper theme – "Virgins," "Freak-out," and "Sacrifice" – have proven beyond doubt that they can get people's attention. Funny video clips, culturally-insensitive creative, or a click that'll virtually deny a hamburger to a Facebook name and thereby earn a coupon for a free, real burger...there's been a torrent of smart, off-the-wall content originating from the company's ad agency, Crispin Porter & Bogusky.

The only problem is that nobody can connect any of it to sales. Not even close.

In the study of evolution, there's a mechanism that allows a species to adapt so completely and exclusively to an ecosystem that it'll be unable to live in any other; worse, even a slight change in those otherwise comfortable environs will amount to a catastrophic challenge to its existence.

I think the Whopper campaigns – going back to the work the company did for its creepy mascot – evidence just such development.

The best, if not the only, thing that anybody can say about these viral/social media campaigns is that they break through the clutter. That's always been a challenge for advertising, even when there was less clutter to break through. In branding" heyday, earning consumer attention was often based on simply interrupting theme. Media was one-way and there weren't many channels (or newspapers, magazines, or radio stations) to choose from, so consumers literally couldn't escape the commercials.

But bothering people was never considered an accomplishment, was it? Nobody got paid for successfully yelling fire in a crowded room. *Branding and marketing had to sell stuff,* which meant using those precious moments gained via interruption to deliver information relevant to buying.

How is it that we now look at marketing and expect the exact opposite?

It's as if the best social media campaigns are those that sell absolutely nothing, but otherwise somehow contribute to the esoteric, absolute value of branding...something so vitally important that it can't be measured by such inconsequential metrics as, well, *sales*?

My gut tells me that we're going to have to come to terms with this disconnect. The chattering class of advocates for the stuff will have to finally put up or shut up, and leave their made-up metrics behind. "Selling" isn't a dirty word, and it can't be wholly left out of the new media marketing equation.

If the junk coming from Burger King is celebrated as smart marketing, then so should a car wreck? Both accomplish pretty much the same thing.

(25) Don't Check Your Guitar

A Canadian musician named Dave Carroll thought it was a good idea to hand off his prized guitar as checked baggage on a United Airlines flight, and then was so incensed when it was returned to him smashed that he recorded a song about it – "United Breaks Guitars" – posted it on YouTube, and got more than 3.5 million views.

Out of the 14,000+ comments he got, I didn't see one that stated the obvious: *How dumb do you have to be to check your guitar?*

Everyone knows the stories, whether true or apocryphal, about baggage handlers: they're rough, careless, and the mouseprint on the tickets absolves them of any liability short of committing murder. American Tourister had a popular TV commercial a while back that featured a suitcase getting mauled by a playful chimp. Even if Carroll had one of those hard cases that was tested to survive a nuclear blast, he should have know it would be stupid to check his computer, collection of crystal glasses, or precious acoustic guitar.

Only he didn't, and instead got pissed off when United refused to ante up to pay for his mistake. It seems that airlines are liable up to $1250/passenger for damage to luggage, not to what might be inside it. United's policy explicitly states that it's not liable "for damage to fragile items."

So Carroll wrote a funny song and shot a funny video, and now we have an illustrative case history on the power of UGC and social media. Or not. Past the page views and colorful comments, I'd ask that we check a few other metrics that might be relevant:

- Did United's bookings go down (or up) while folks were tuning into YouTube?

- Did its complaints go up (or down) from travelers with baggage damage issues?

- Did travelers learn anything new about United (or air travel in general)?

Does the popularity of the video illustrate the power of individual consumers over large, anonymous organizations? If so, then the measures should be some change in United's policy (which hasn't changed at all, as far as I can tell).

So what does it tell us? I say that United missed a chance to ride the wave, and get some free exposure:

- It should have videotaped its own response (after all, one silly song deserves another). Maybe Ms. Irlweg, who Carroll named in his video as the most-unhelpful customer rep, could have riffed on all the objects she was relieved he hadn't chosen to check.

- How about starting a contest for other people to post videos about what they love or hate about the airline? Let people register and get frequent flier miles for participating; there's really no such thing as bad publicity, is there?

- Carroll is debuting a second video about his conversations with United, so why didn't the company offer to co-create it with him? Clearly, he sees this as his track to fame, and he seems like a good guy, so why not co-opt him?

I'm not sure there'll be any lasting impact for this swift exchange of UGC and viewer commentary, any more than the swapping of Iran tweets resulted in more than convenient, and passing, indignation. Well, maybe after all is said and done, there's one lesson that will have been learned:

Don't check your guitar.

(26) Ford's Confused Conversation

Ford has recruited 100 "young, web-savvy" consumers to drive its Fiesta subcompact for six months and then chatter about it online, in hopes that they'll serve as "opinion leaders" and "build a collective of digital storytellers" a full year before the car is available for sale.

It's a big idea to start the sales conversation many moons before dealerships start twisting arms, but I fear that Ford has got the substance of it all wrong.

The gurus who make money selling these sorts of campaigns see it as a way of pre-populating the web with reviews, *a la* the hotel reviews many travel sites provide. It's a fact that consumers value the opinions of their fellows, and often find the information more credible that that which is normally provided by brand marketers. One of Ford's reviewers shot a wacky video to qualify for the campaign (it was a contest, of sorts) that has been watched almost 300,000 times on YouTube. Reaching 300,000 people for free is really cool, so the participants for the campaign were chosen by a combination of 1) how active they were online, and 2) how creative.

This isn't really a conversation, though, is it? Since each reviewer has been *schwagged* with a car, gas, and insurance, it's not likely that many of them will aggressively slam the Fiesta. A vast majority of the posts will be "slice of life" fluff, so it may not necessarily tell anybody anything useful (or compelling). Lots of it will be consciously creative, or at least aspire to be funnier or edgier than it turns out to be.

In other words, Ford has outsourced its pre-launch advertising campaign to:

- People who aren't really capable of producing good advertising
- A medium that demands that nothing get advertised on it anyway.

I get it. The goal is to get people to get other people to talk about the videos and blog posts, vs. necessarily talking about something as humdrum as a car. This is one of those marvelously nonsense, self-referential arguments for social media: the most important dialogue must focus on whatever is least important to the business.

You remember those commercials for Nissan's failed Sentra launch a while back, with the slacker guy living in his car? Multiply that by 100 people, few of whom will be anywhere near as funny or engaging as Nissan's faux blogger, and you'll have the brilliant insight behind Ford's Fiesta campaign.

I still don't quite get why otherwise smart marketers continue to confuse social conversation with distracting noise, however momentarily entertaining the cacophony might be. Imagine if Ford had elected to actually respect its Generation Whatever would-be customers, and constructed a way to actually talk to and with them prior to the product launch?

- It could have been relevant to consumers, not as an entertainment vehicle (no pun intended), but focused on functional things that matter...fuel efficiency, durability, whatever. It would be a far greater creative challenge to come up with program(s) that made these qualities engaging and interactive, instead of opting for yucks and buzz.

- But with relevance comes potential utility, so the effort could have involved specific uses and applications for participation. Maybe would-be consumers could sign-up to do things and somehow "earn" discounts on the ultimate purchase? Perhaps the campaign could have provided information, in some creative and compelling way, to get people to hold off from contemplated purchases until the Fiesta is available.

- Because, ultimately, it's not the conversation that matters as much as the transactions during it, whether of the car, or add-ons, or services. Couldn't potential customers have been involved in helping design aspects of the offering – music downloads, service deals, even novel pricing or financing models – that they could then transact when available?

It's just too damn easy to aspire to hipness, being cute, and coming across as current or topical. The Detroit automakers have spent literally billions over the past few years alone trying every which way from Sunday to do it, and they've failed miserably.

I fear that even if lots of people see the Fiesta posts, and are entertained more than once, it still won't get Ford any closer to selling cars.

(27) This Spot Makes Me Puke

Microsoft continues to stumble along its doomed quest for cool with a series of Internet videos that make absolutely no sense. One spot was so incomprehensibly bad that popular outcry got it yanked.

The campaign is purportedly targeted at Millennials, who are obviously defined by their shared disinterest in anything like functional reality, honesty, or good taste; each spot is a combination faux public interest message/Chris

Hansen-like expose, revealing people embarrassing themselves as they suffer various web afflictions that IE8 can cure. The spots have acronym titles, like "F.O.M.S.," for "fear of missing something." A campaign landing page promises a donation, amounting to approximately $1.15, to Feeding America each time IE8 gets downloaded.

Sound just exquisitely mixed-up and wrong-headed? Yup, sure is. And it didn't have to be:

- A cause is a good thing. Linking downloads to something meaningful is totally legitimate; Microsoft just chose to blow it up entirely in executing the program. Imagine if there'd been some understandable goal, like "feed a million people for a year?" Imagine if downloaders could prompt larger contributions by doing more, like participating in polls, or even getting involved directly? A cause-related marketing program without such qualities just reeks of insincerity.

- Funny videos can be useful. They just have to be relevant to the intended viewers, and being so means providing some connection other than artsy corollaries of a fart joke. Does anybody think that Internet browsing is cool or funny? There must be better, still fun ways to illustrate functional benefits of IE8; getting would-be users engaged in relevant content would have done much more for the brand.

- Talking about branding isn't branding. I love the circular logic that drives campaigns like this: the branding strategy is to get people to talk about the branding strategy. Ultimately, the Microsoft videos tell us nothing about I8, nor does the Feeding America tie-in give us anything compelling us to action. It's all about how edgy and creative its marketing can be. Download or use IE8? Yeah, whatever.

One fellow bulber suggested that Microsoft shot the puke spot with the specific intention of prompting an outcry (a tactic pulled out of the 'ol "there's no such thing as bad publicity" playbook). I don't think the company is willing to take such risks, though the segment is egregiously bad.

Getting attention with the puke spot simply forces the question that all the other spots similarly fail to answer: why should anybody care?

(28) Shooting The Messenger

Late last month, Virgin Atlantic fired 13 flight attendants for making disparaging comments about safety and passengers in a Facebook forum. British

Airways followed a few days later to punish employees who posted references to travelers as "smelly" and "annoying."

As the proponents of social media tell it, these were examples of the necessity for companies to:

- Have better rules about employee blogging.

- Monitor more closely the places where they might talk.

- More aggressively participate in said media, from a corporate perspective.

Here's a novel, alternate idea: *fix your reality problems*. Skip thinking the answer is to do a better job of tail wagging, and ask different questions of the dog.

It's not a secret that airline passengers are often both smelly and obnoxious. Anybody who has to fly more than one a year will tell you so. I had a flight delayed earlier this week because a passenger couldn't find room to store her suitcase in the cabin, and needed to let everyone within earshot know just how unhappy she was (and that we were all complicit offenders). I've sat next to people removing nail polish, and others eating giant pizzas. And maintenance, like service, is directly dependent on the available time and resources to deliver it, so it's more than likely that some lesser priority items might sometimes (or often) slip. One of the fired attendants referenced cockroaches in plane galleys. Would any of us be surprised to see that?

So the airline employees weren't fired because they used social media. They were fired because they told the truth, and social media just happened to be the way they did it. Whatever they'd posted online had probably been the topics of face-to-face conversations for a long, long time.

If the marketers at Virgin or BA had any self-respect, they'd refuse to act as the media Gestapo, and decline to spend any more company money outsourcing enforcement policies to external mercenaries. Instead, the real marketing challenge is a business challenge, and the marketers should help their employers see the real problems that need fixing:

- You can't cut staff and expect fewer people to maintain the same (let alone better) service, whether serving drinks or cleaning the planes.

- You can't declare bag or food charge policies, and then expect the employees to absorb the negative reactions from passengers.

- Plane turn-around schedules can't be so tight that plane clean-up has to start 20 minutes before the things actually land.

- You can't let passengers treat airplane cabins as their own personal space, with no obvious rules for their behavior. Remember, these are the people who don't stop at stop signs because they're talking on their phones. They cut lines at Starbucks. There need to be standards posted and enforced.

While I know that every external factor has made it nearly impossible for airlines to be profitable, they've done their very best to make sure that their employees fail. No amount of branding communications (or policing by the people trying to provide service) can or should change that.

Figure out ways to make airplane cabins more pleasant, and get rid of the cockroaches in the galleys, and there'll be no more negative posts on Facebook. That's the real branding challenge, and the message everyone needs to hear. What the airlines have been doing so far is shooting the messenger.

(29) Too Much vs. Too Little

Yahoo's new limits on user data retention and Facebook's latest row over faux college groups illustrate the bizarro-world conflict between too little and too much information in search, social media, and online life in general.

Why is it that companies know too much about us, and we know too little about one another? Shouldn't it be the other way around?

Yahoo is going to delete after 90 days some of the personally identifiable search behavior data it collects. These are the breadcrumb trails that we all leave when we look something up on the web, and the standard is to hold onto the stuff for at least a year or so...because it's commercial gold: by tracking and correlating the queries you type into your computer, companies like Google, Microsoft, and Yahoo can extrapolate tons of conclusions about your lifestyle, and your interests.

This allows them to sell access to your eyeballs to companies that might sell you stuff that you might want. So two people entering in the search term "tuna fish" might get two different sets of paid results, depending on how the engines have predicted the likelihood of one commercial interest exploiting your interest vs. another.

We get sold every step of the way. It's called *providing a better search experience.*

Conversely, the latest row on Facebook involves a company setting up faux college group pages, with the intention of capturing names for some similarly nefarious (i.e. commercial) purpose. The rise of social media has been driven by people interacting with one another based on at least some shared tidbit of information (interest, gender, topic, education, etc.), yet little of it is certified as authentic. We interact with one another online almost wholly as anonymous trollers, identifiable only by the stuff we choose to share. While a search engine can map your behavior with near-actuarial certainty, I know nothing about you when we "meet" online.

Detached from the responsibility of identity, participants in social media can be whomever (or whatever) they want to be. So can companies, which continually try to exploit the medium with faux individuals, pages, and groups (that person in a user forum who won't stop waxing poetic about the virtues of Microsoft Vista is probably a paid agent).

The common retort of the word-of-mouth community is that the crowd will eventually out the violators, whether individual participants or entire groups (as in the case of the latest Facebook heresy). I'll eventually discover that you're not who you say you are, or that the community I've joined is a scam. There are no secrets, ultimately, on the Internet; the crowd deserves your constant trust.

But it begs a central question: *really?*

The vast, interconnected enormity of the Internet comes down to two extremes, in my thinking:

1. You either build very closed communities, in which you can certify that the members are really who they say they are (and are there for the reasons they've revealed), or

2. You outsource your trust to the most authentically anonymous crowds possible (that, by definition, are too generic to have any POV or bias to manipulate you, or if one emerged, you'd know it).

I'd put the big search engines and many online social groups somewhere between, and I'm not sure it's a sustainable place to be. I wonder if people are going to trend to the extremes of the experience continuum. If so, while it's great that search engines like Yahoo promise to limit data exploitation, and that faux communities or individuals will ultimately get outed, it might not be enough.

(30) Is Second Life Dead?

The virtual world Second Life ("SL") has been in the news recently, announcing some high-profile executive changes, and a new policy to help users filter out mature content.

I think the thing might be dead already, only nobody knows it yet.

For those of you who've managed to avoid the hype over the past few years, SL is a virtual world – a landscape, replete with mountains, oceans, and lots of places on which people can build things like houses, temples, and stores – in which members can appear and interact as cartoon characters, called "avatars." The business was conceived primarily as a real estate company, which provided the land on which people could do things (and which could be created endlessly for little incremental cost to the company, Linden Labs).

The model is a miracle because it all but invented the idea of purely digital assets having value. The primary activities in the SL world are 1) avatars flirting with one another, and 2) the sale of digital buildings, hairdos, clothes, and special body parts, all intended to help improve the experience (see activity 1). Concurrently, some companies have bought land on SL and done everything from setting up virtual showrooms and sampling opportunities, to designing meeting rooms and asking employees (or job applicants) to use SL for meetings. They've even sold virtual merchandise, like logo T-shirts or gym shoes for avatars to wear.

Linden says that user-to-user monetary transactions could reach $450 million this year. Remember, these are all virtual bits of electrons on computer screens, nothing more. I should be such a failure. It's amazing stuff.

Got it. So now what?

There are few things that you can accomplish via SL that you can't do via any number of other technologies, from IM and Facebook, to VoIP conferencing, mobile texting, or playing World of Warcraft or EVE Online. The idea that SL lets you do them through your animated and often life-like avatar is totally cool, as is the creation and transfer of those digital assets.

Further, it turns out that technology platforms need to have relevance and utility for the real world, just as all of those other interactive technologies offer. I can us IM for work, or VoIP to stay in touch with my relatives in Sweden. Buying virtual products within SL does little for my business in the real world, if anything. SL's benefits, like an online MMORPG, are inclusive of experience, and exclusive of any external application.

SL remains a technology platform more than a community, or a place. And it's certainly not a game. But it could be. The fundamental drivers of game experience are the same as those that give real life its meaning (or at least resonance to moments within it): sense of direction, responsibility, risk-and-reward, second chances and, overall, purpose. Experiences don't have to be recognized as games consciously to be fulfilling, as any coupon-clipper, sale shopper, or parent striving to outwit her kids will tell you.

Gaming is a strategic model before it's the label for a product or service. And, in the instance of SL (and even if users can invent games within it), it's ultimately a destination without structure, content, or purpose.

Imagine a different approach, such as the avatars of SL organized into actual countries...with citizenship responsibilities, work requirements, and all the other opportunities and detritus of experience that constitute, well, living. Citizenship would mean that people had actual roles in their communities, and had things they actually had to do other than show up, float around, and buy new jewelry. Forget being a bland, pointless simulacra of real life; it would be it's own life, a true "second life," rich with consequences, continuity, and all that other stuff that differentiates stuff that matters from stuff that doesn't.

A fundamental premise of these countries would have to be some limit on resources, so there were constraints (rules) in which the communities operated. So you could just see the fights between businesses, or the political campaigns and efforts. SL would become something that people actually lived.

Without a plan for how people will truly live there in the future, I wonder whether the idea isn't already dead?

Just For Fun: Leap Moments

I've been obsessed lately with the frequency and duration of leap moments.

This is a term of my own making, and I'm referring to those moments when whatever it is you're doing is put on hold, paused, or there's otherwise a few minutes that don't seem to belong to anyone. Like when the line gets longer than a few people at the Starbucks or fast food counter. Or when you're waiting for your order to be fulfilled. Sitting on an airplane within a stone's throw of the gate, but you can't get off for 10 minutes because nobody's there to open it. An elevator trip that makes a dozen stops via slow-moving doors. You know, exceptions. Interludes. Leap moments.

They usually occur when something that's supposed to occur doesn't, or doesn't happen fast enough. They also usually involve a group of people, aggregated in physical space, and often arise because of their presence (i.e. too many people trying to do something at the same time). Leap moments are somewhat predictable, and a fairly regular fixture in our supposedly hyper-paced lives. *They're like extra time*, or moments out of time.

So, thinking as any good marketer should, I wonder how could we exploit them?

There's not much happening on this front so far. When people wait on the telephone ("we're experiencing unusually high call volume"), it's common practice to throw advertising at them, since they're quite literally captives. But waiting on hold is a solitary experience, and there are far better ways to engage with folks than subjecting them to recorded ads via IVR. Yet this approach is the most common tool used when folks are similarly held captive in geophysical real space, too.

I choose to define the marketing opportunity differently, and focus on the qualities of those moments that people share, even as they do their best to ignore one another (iPod volume, anyone?).

I wonder:

- Would people want to play a game of some sort?

- How about some activity that earned them benefits that could be used moments later (i.e. could waiting be so incentivized that folks would look forward to them)?

- Maybe these impromptu aggregations of consumers could be focus groups, or information-sharing experiences? I mean, isn't standing in line a *de facto* social activity...or could be?

- Why not simply (and basically) use them as opportunities to communicate with people on substance or some other quality (other than throwing ads at them that they didn't ask to see or hear)?

Again, right now, these moments are exceptions – almost as if businesses don't know what to do with people – and yet they are common enough that they should get incorporated into the overall brand planning. I'm not thinking logos and marketing, though, but rather working to figure out what might your consumers want to do with a few found leap moments?

There's another possible approach, of course: *stop making us wait*

Chapter Four
The Reality of Reputation

In case you didn't notice it, almost every public and commercial establishment blew up in 2009.

Some of the explosions were obvious, like the disappearance of some of the world's leading names in finance. Others were simmering and continuous, like the nagging public distrust on issues like global warming or healthcare, or the policy responses to the economic meltdown. Corporate reputations all over the world suffered on a variety of fronts.

For a planet that is evermore wrapped in the knowing embrace of instantaneous communications, networked conversation, and access to literally infinite amounts of information, people seemed to agree less, distrust more, and rely on a shrinking list of truths in 2009.

The more we know, the less we believe. I think the two phenomena are related.

Our institutions were slow to respond to this reality; there's no better example than what happened with financial firms, whose very structural foundations were called into question early in the year. Cold, hard facts proved old processes and certitudes to be no longer reliable, and individual investors lost untold amounts of money. How did financial firms respond? They bought expensive branding that effectively told people "don't worry, be happy." Everything would be fine, if only everyone would go back to doing what they used to do. The firms announced no changes in behavior or reporting. The structural causes (or enablers) of the meltdown were never addressed, at least not publicly.

Didn't you sense a disconnect, especially when some of the firms started revealing immense profits (and the return of executive bonuses)?

A similar disconnect with the truth was evidenced when corporations claimed that consumers should simply "trust" the incremental stasis of corporate good works. Worried about global warming? Your friendly neighborhood oil company was on it in 2009, with glossy commercials of its scientists busy at work solving the problem. Bothered that agriculture businesses made oodles of profits while a large chunk of humanity starved? No worries, because they contributed to charity. Product tampering got you spooked? The brands promised to never let it happen...again.

Credibility is going to be a major differentiator between public and private institutions in the coming years. People can connect the dots, or believe that they can, and the fact that they're rejecting most traditional forms of marketing could have something to do with the fact there's rarely much truth contained in it. Reputation has moved out of the hands of corporate spokespeople, image makers, and symbolic good works, and into reality.

I firmly believe this trend toward suspicion and argument-as-debate is going to be with us for a while, so your challenge is going to be how to walk the talk before you choose to talk about your walk. Here are 10 conclusions from the year's posts:

1. Tell the truth. I know it's a simple, silly thing to say, but you'd be surprised how many businesses (and government entities) fail to do so. If your product destroys ancient forests but makes life more meaningful for your employees and customers, tell people about it. Be creatively nuts with it, but use your abilities to communicate reality. That's a harder task than trying to obfuscate it.

2. Realize that the truth is 'out there' whether you tell it or not. I think this Internet-thing is here to stay, don't you? If you don't embed and otherwise connect your every corporate gesture with the context of information available to your audience, you might as well be talking to yourself.

3. Symbols are just symbols; they have no inherent meaning, and all of the communications tools that used to attach ideas to them aren't as reliable as they used to be. This is the substance behind much of the backlash against "greenwashing," for instance. Think actions, not just how you'll communicate them.

4. Don't make things harder than they have to be. Many of the inputs into social media are simply facts. Create and distribute more truth, and don't let the format hold you back (or occupy too much of your time).

5. If you have a problem, talk less, and act more. How you "respond" to a PR crisis isn't about your communications or word count on a social media dashboard.

6. Reputation is an outcome of business practices, not a campaign from marketing, or a CSR program.

7. As such, your corporate reputation isn't something that "is," but rather something your business does all the time. You "repute" every time your organization does something (or fails to do something).

8. I think you really want, to reexamine your branding; specifically as it relates to the operational reality of your business. Some of the brands hurt worst over the past few years were those that made declarations (explicit or implicit) that weren't supported by the behavior of the company.

9. What are your specific, objective metrics of reputation? There are many meaningful systems for tracking reputation, but can you come up with a few variables (and/or ratios) that are direct outcomes with meaning to your business? What you think it means may not be what it means in 2010 and beyond.

10. Oh yeah, tell the truth, and then substantiate it with real business actions, not marketing.

Here are 10 essays on looking at reputation in a new way:

(31) The Confusion of Good Works

Boeing's CEO for commercial airplanes wrote an op-ed piece in this weekend's *Wall Street Journal* that started with this declaration: "Addressing climate change is a particularly difficult challenge for commercial aviation."

The rest of the piece went on to forcefully argue that it's not going to happen unless government makes it profitable and, perhaps indirectly and more importantly, it's not Boeing's job.

What a shock...*a company telling the truth.* I think that doing so does more for its brand than any amount of politically correct "we're working together to save the planet" marketing blather it could have run.

Sure, the piece is headlined with the disingenuous "How Boeing Fights Climate Change," and there are throwaway references to how the efficiency of commercial jets has risen 70%, which has meant a 70% reduction in carbon emissions per mile. See, Boeing is fighting climate change!

No, it isn't, and it shouldn't have to. Boeing is in the business of manufacturing and servicing commercial airplanes, among its many other businesses. It has a fiduciary responsibility to its shareholders and investors, and hopes to gainfully employee its workers as long as there's work to be had. It's a nearly-perfect B2B endeavor, as there's little pull strategy for consumer fliers. You'd no more feel the need to choose which elevator brand took you up and down in a high-rise, or whether concrete sold under a particular name was used to repave your favorite road.

Whatever mentions it makes about the well-being of society or the planet in its mission statement, values, or other *consultantspeak* it might have framed on its office walls, is definitely followed like that game you play when you read a Chinese fortune cookie: adding "in between the sheets" after whatever it is, Boeing's value statements have the same requirement as any other company to include, however implicitly, "as long as it makes money for us."

Its CEO says as much as he outlines the ways government can help Boeing help the environment:

- Focus on efficiency standards broadly instead of mandating specific emissions limits, so as to encourage innovation.

- Improve runway and flight path management so there's less idling time, or whatever it's called, along with less fuel burned in the air.

- Incentivize farmers and refiners to grow biofuels for airlines to use.

In other words, doing the right thing means incentivizing it, financially. Don't rely on them expending shareholders' wealth in the name of some abstract planetary good, or because someone on the board wants to get on the cover of *Fortune* (or anonymous posts in a chatroom demand it).

The easier thing to do would also be the most common: namely, hire some smart marketers and publicists, and come up with some symbolic gesture, like a donation or other good work. Commit $x and then spend many more dollars promoting the hell out of it. There's an entire racket – calling itself "corporate social responsibility," or "CSR" – that gives companies the excuse to claim to do good in order to realize some branding benefit. Think cigarette companies supporting the ballet and Public Television, only now an entire industry exists to support those activities.

There's an inherent disconnect...no, a dishonesty...between the explicit requirements of businesses to make profits, and the implicit expectations we put on them to do things beside that. CSR treats good works as a marketing and branding strategy, almost as if it's apart or aside from the base, mercenary activities of the business.

Three cheers to Boeing for cutting through the confusion, however unintended and imperfectly. If we want commercial jetliners to help save the environment, our government needs to find ways to help them make money. If more companies actually told the truth about the sometime conflicts between "good business" and "good works," maybe we'd believe more often what they have to say the rest of the time.

(32) Wal-Mart Should See More Green

I can't believe I'm saying it, but Wal-Mart deserves more money.

I think it should get paid for its green initiatives, which seem a lot more sincere and real than any of the CSR marketing nonsense that passes for environmental responsibility at other companies. It started down a path in 2005 to remake its business based on principles of sustainability, with some frightening huge long-term goals:

- Running operations solely on renewable energy.
- Creating zero waste.
- Selling only products that sustain the earth's resources and environment.

It also shared its intentions with its suppliers, which dared them into embracing similar goals, if not explicitly or for their own businesses overall, at least for the products and services they hoped to sell in Wal-Mart stores. P&G ramped up development and production of concentrated laundry detergent. GE starting making lots more fluorescent light bulbs.

Now, people can have legitimate issues with Wal-Mart. Employee salaries and benefits are contentious points, as is union organizing. The *uber*-economic role it plays in replacing local, inefficient manufacturers and suppliers with distant, efficient vendors has massive implications for communities (its provision of low prices to consumers requires them to unwittingly stop being producers). You could even question the motives behind its green initiative.

But I would ask why? Who cares what its leadership is thinking? As a matter of fact, let's just presume that Wal-Mart does nothing for the greater good. Altruism isn't a word that appears in its employee handbooks. Building a sustainable business, and selling sustainable economy products, is pure, mercenary contrivance, intended to do nothing but enrich Wal-Mart and its shareholders.

Good. That's exactly the sort of corporate responsibility we need. Skip all the branding nonsense about "having a conversation about our energy future," or symbolic donations to charitable causes. The real drivers of brand equity don't reside in the imaginations of communicators, but rather in the spreadsheets of business operators. We should be less concerned with what companies say, and more with what they do.

And that's not just when it comes to green initiatives. Any claim of a product or service attribute should have its basis in some actual thing(s) a company actually does.

At least on this issue, Wal-Mart is a company to emulate. I wonder why it's not doing a better job driving consumers with the info. It could probably see more green for all the green it's seeing.

(33) Bad Investments

GMAC has changed its name to "Ally," AIG has become "AIU," and we're supposed to think there's a difference.

The new branding comes on the heels of some very aggressive communications from many of the survivors of the financial meltdown, most of which delivers a variation on a theme that could broadly be expressed as "we've been in business forever, and we care about you, so trust us."

So was the breakdown of investment ratings, actual returns, and the implicit (and sometimes explicit) promises of suitability and reliability *just a blip?*

Has the last year of news been an exception that we can happily forget? Did the evaporation of zillions in value have no effect on policy or procedures at the financial firms still around? What a miracle of branding this is. Financial institutions are in a state of denial, and they're asking consumers to go along for the ride.

I know I'm a dim bulb, but I really don't get it. Remember when the toy companies got caught with lead paint and other product defects a few years back? Consumers were subjected to the usual corporate communications blather – investigations, cooperating with authorities, and a collective company-wide shock – and then reminded that the brands stood for things better, and more reliable (and thus were somehow not responsible).

Checklists were rechecked, and mention of an errant factory here or there ("there" being China, or somewhere else far away) made the rounds on the Internet, but then the story disappeared. Crisis resolved. If the toymakers are doing anything substantively different today than they were before the problems got national attention, they've not bothered to tell anyone. My suspicion is that they've spent the time finding new ways to shave costs, circumvent minor details of regulation, and otherwise get away with making as much money as they can. Just like normal.

Does Mattel truly stand for safe products today? Of course not. Similarly, Bank of America, MorganStanleySmithBarney, and the other financial firms blowing lots of money on brand image advertising aren't any safer, better, or reliably different than they were before the meltdown. If they were, don't you think they'd tell us?

This approach to branding is condescending, at best, and an outright insult to our intelligence, more likely.

As with any other crisis, there's an opportunity for financial institutions to truly differentiate and achieve real, meaningful positions in the marketplace. But they have to do things differently in order to be perceived as different. New policies, programs, and products. More transparency on how decisions and recommendations are made. Better engagement and education with investors, both large and small.

I'm suspicious of the companies that are making the most noise; they should be doing things other than marketing the return of the Status Quo. Their glossy branding nonsense just looks like a bad investment.

(34) Peanut Butter's Bad Reputation

The peanut butter recall is expanding, and now includes some Clif bars, General Mills products, Kellogg cookies, Keebler crackers, and a swath of private label products. Little Debbie voluntarily recalled its peanut butter crackers, just in case.

A lot of other brand names have vociferously declared that their products are "safe," have no connection to the culprit factory, or simply haven't been named in the recall.

Are you reassured?

The days of companies issuing statements that carry any legitimacy are long gone. Armies of lawyers and PR experts dictate scope and content, and most announcements are intended to announce whatever is deemed in the best interests of the corporation. Rarely, if ever, does this overlap with any lay definition of right, let alone consumer expectations for transparency or clarity.

It's worse, considering you'd have thought that safety was an implicit brand promise – "by the way, our stuff won't kill you" – so whether impacted by the recall or not, aren't *all* the makers of peanut butter products sullied by the mere fact that they share a base commodity?

This isn't a PR crisis, it's an operational crisis. Consumers need guarantees that their peanut butter is safe, which requires that they understand the processes involved in getting the commodity into candy, crackers, and sandwiches. And that means talking to them like adults.

For starters, there's a big, gaping disconnect that no brand is addressing: how does tainted stuff get all the way into the distribution chain that they only way it's caught is when some consumer dies from it? How are supplies checked? What certification gets passed from vendor to vendor? When are samples rechecked? What makes explicit the brand commitment that people can eat (or use) stuff with confidence?

These answers aren't a press release announcement or post on a web site, but rather a detailed exploration of the supply chain, and then a creative, marketing approach to making it relevant and useful to consumers:

- Get the operations folks identifying the processes that deliver certainties that matter to end-users, not just meeting the bare minimums of regulation

- Then get the marketers doing something other than distracting people, or giving consumers nonsense social media campaigns...and invent ways to augment those operational certainties, like getting producers and consumers involved (how about social tools used as early warning systems for product issues.

I don't think we're going to see any of this, unfortunately. The peanut butter issue is going to be viewed as a crisis of reputation, not reality, and consumers will get lots of communications blather from the people who normally produce that stuff.

If they respond accordingly, they'll stop eating peanut butter.

(35) Another Oil Shock

Archer Daniels Midland ("ADM") just announced that its 1Q09 profit more than doubled, due primarily to the success of its oilseeds processing unit.

Much like the winner/loser dynamics of the fossil fuels business, there are some challenges inherent in delivering shockingly great profits in a global food marketplace that is also seeing record price hikes, and a commensurate rise in malnutrition and starvation.

I wonder how ADM will incorporate its success into a believable and relevant brand narrative.

Seed oil is an ingredient used in the manufacture soap, cosmetics, and food (from feeding livestock, to keeping your spaghetti from sticking to your plate), and ADM markets it via various *Soylent-Green-spooky* brand names, like NuSun and Superb. It cited higher commodity costs in making these products as the driver of its higher prices. Clearly, it was able to find room for increased margins on those sales, and the marketplace didn't blink.

There is nothing wrong with making oodles of money, of course. It's what businesses are supposed to do, and a quick survey of ADM's website reveals that it pays the requisite "taxes" in activities that constitute corporate social responsibility ("CSR"), like donating money in Africa. It also promotes the various mission statements, codes of conduct, rules for a sustainable supply chain, and environmental stewardship that vocal interest groups demand. You name an issue, and there's a symbolic "give" on the site.

I think it's missing an opportunity to integrate its CSR into its business strategy and branding. And I suspect that its latest financial success will beg the issue.

What it doesn't want to do is mimic the fossil fuels companies, which make similar gestures to the issues that its polling and surveys say consumers care about. Those inconsequentially minuscule efforts, and the giant branding budgets spent promoting them, only serve to highlight the disconnect inherent in many corporate approaches to their markets:

- The "good works" conflict with the obvious purpose and performance of the businesses.
- This is why there's no real money behind them.

No wonder nobody believes the oil companies when they declare that they're working to find alternatives to fossil fuels. They're not, and Exxon-

Mobil said as much in a rare moment of honesty as it defeated various CSR-inspired shareholder proposals at its annual meeting earlier this year.

And that's OK, as long as the brand finds a way to tell people the truth instead. So here are three ideas that ADM might want to immediately consider as it plans its branding for '09:

1. Metrics for business that include CSR measures: The responsibility tab on its website is nice and fairly robust, but it still seems like a diversion, or an addition, to the core of its business...even if it's not. It comes across that way, and it's highlighted when a quarterly report reveals record profits. Why not find ways to incorporate metrics for its good works performance with the metrics for its profit performance. "Save x # of kids from starvation," for instance. Or some other bold numbers?

2. Context for its good works: Stated as absolutes, the declarations of its supply chain efforts or charitable giving are hard to fathom: are they important or inconsequential, in light of the company's overall performance? Instead of presenting its CSR as information available if asked (the proverbial learn more links), why not find ways to proactively present it consistently, over time?

3. Link it to selling activities: Ultimately, responsibility isn't an activity or campaign, it's a business strategy (or it's a happy lie). The missives from the company's CEO suggest that it matters, so prove it...find ways to operationalize it, and build it into how projects are proposed, contracts are priced, and partners are selected. Don't give money away, but rather demand that you make it while being responsible.

The branding challenge for ADM is broad, in that it's just too easy to juxtapose its record profits with the latest news reports of soaring food prices. Everybody can see it. So perhaps if it more aggressively incorporated what seem to be its many good works into its outbound brand, it might prevent, or at least lessen, the negative fallout?

Otherwise, I worry it'll soon see the backlash of another oil shock.

(36) IBM Kills Trees to Save the Planet

IBM's latest corporate branding efforts for its environmental impact appears on full-page newspaper ads. Or maybe it's a campaign to promote its green consulting services. It doesn't matter. The strategy is intended to kill trees, whether explicitly or not.

If you actually take the time to read the ads, they're actually full of really good stuff. It turns out that technology can be used to do green relevant things without necessarily being particularly green themselves. Think of a giant thermostat, like for a city: power grids are as leaky and lame as an inflatable swimming pool. If you control streetlights more intelligently, cars spend less time idling (and are more fuel efficient). Better modeling of purchasing needs can mean that stores can spend less money on energy, like for keeping storage spaces hot or cold.

The idea that technology can do green things is pretty powerful, and it's a great commercial for a solutions offering from IBM. It could be the basis for it to claim that it cares about the environment, as you can credibly interpret its efficiency activities as being fundamentally green.

So why newspaper ads (and the incomprehensible creative)? The visuals are abstract graphics, the text is excruciatingly long, and the eventual call-to-action is a lame invite: "Join us and see what others are thinking."

This branding should be electronic, wasting electrons ripped from the fabric of space-time, and not a finite resource (recycling notwithstanding). It should be unavoidably obvious, which would mean illustrative imagery, not graphics courtesy of Paul Klee. The text should be simple and direct, declaring facts instead of weaving around and among them. And there should be some central focus for participation by consumers (and/or whomever IBM is trying to reach).

Imagine a checklist to apply to your own friendly, local utility, to ascertain if it's using the most advanced or effective technology to manage energy distribution/use. Maybe an online tool for businesses to share tech solutions to improve energy use or savings...maybe even a contest?

There are lots of ways to do things to communicate the idea. Running abstract corporate branding ads isn't one of them. All it tells us is that IBM is willing to kill trees in order to tell us it's helping save the planet.

(37) Mexico's Branding Nightmare

Salmonella. Drug violence. Now swine flu. You think Mexico's development and tourism marketers are having a few sleepless nights?

Only this nightmare is real.

It has always been a contrivance to think we could separate, say, the branding of farm produce, from the realities of where and how it's grown, or present imagery of luxury resorts and pristine beaches that didn't somehow trigger recollections of drug war casualties pictured on the Internet. American consumers have, in general, deluded themselves into pretending that the miasma of life for millions of poor, ignored, and exploited Mexicans wouldn't affect us across the border, in spite of every effort to claim that the only problem was that too many of them wanted to live here.

Tourism is all about marketing fantasy, just like economic development relies on a large does of hope. We're supposed to look at those empty beaches in resort ads and suppress the fact that we know the coastline is likely filled with fellow pale, flabby tourists (like us). Manufacturers need to close one eye to the way workers live, or are treated on the job, or they'd never source or buy products anywhere but Iowa.

Marketing relies on us maintaining this separation, this double-think, and uses tools like creative rationales, excuses, and symbolism to obfuscate or distract. Only sometimes reality catches up. So what should Mexico do about it?

The Old School Approach would be to do absolutely nothing. This nightmare will end, and a new day will dawn, once again filled with hapless and willing tourists and businesses. Human beings have memories a tad bit longer than gnats, and we prefer the happy comfort of our well-practiced doublethink (see above). Any proactive or additional communicating on negatives such as poisoning, murder, and disease wouldn't do much for the brand; other than extend the bad news. So cancel whatever marketing you can. Better to hunker down, and wait for the troubles to pass.

A new approach would be to consider that this Internet thing is going to be with us for a while, and that the nature of how people become aware and make decisions about things is not like it used to be.

Imagine if the top marketers of Mexico's leading resorts and exporters got together, and committed to figuring out what they needed in order to restore confidence in their brands?

No, not come up with some creative nonsense, but address first the operational, substantive hurdles...the messy, inconvenient facts that keep popping up, and then finding eternal life online. They would come up with must-do recommendations for their employers, and for their government, and then they could go public with them, so as to enlist engagement and support from the larger community. The creative marketing-types wouldn't even be allowed in the room, but instead hired once the substantive changes needed to get communicated.

Do food producers need another layer of third-party inspection? Should factories have webcams to witness behavior, or should worker treatment get linked more closely to the parts and finished goods that get shipped? Could the vectors for transmission of swine flu (not to mention the factors that allowed for its genesis) require major, meaningful changes to public health laws and enforcement?

I know, the likelihood of such a confab is next to zero, and the prospect for any such recommendations getting put into practice even less so. But I'm not sure Mexico's marketers have a chance to wake up from their branding nightmare without it.

(38) Equity, Schmecklity

Dow Chemical Co. is going to whack 5,000 employees, or 11% of its total workforce, and will tell another 6,000 contractors to sit on their hands until further notice.

So much for the human element.

"The Human Element" is the corporate branding campaign that Dow has been running since 2006. It's gloriously beautiful and thematically broad...an ethnically-diverse series of facial close-ups, positioned next to vague declarations about the importance of community, the environment, and global happiness. I'm sure the company spent many millions on it. The campaign has earned Dow high praise in the communities that tend to praise such expenditures: one branding apologist declared that Dow's brand equity had soared in 2007, growing 34% to account for 16.22% of the company's market capitalization. A global PR campaign based on the branding was a success because it helped Dow "build new and often stronger relationships with stakeholders."

While its marketers were busy delivering their ideal of the brand (and congratulating one another), the marketplace changed.

Energy prices went up, demand went down, and the financing of Dow's business activities (ongoing, as well as at least one very pricey acquisition) got a lot harder. So now it's shuttering 200 factories, and discarding lots of people.

What's this going to do to the company's branding, I wonder?

The strange thing is that Dow is actually a responsible business. No, not by the nonsense measures of the corporate social responsibility marketing crowd, but for real. Sure, it makes modest, mostly symbolic commitments to do good in the world, and then promotes the hell out of them...what company can resist, right? But Dow made a business strategy decision a few years ago, encapsulated in a document entitled "2015 Sustainability Goals." It's a guide to how it intends to lower the social and environmental impacts of its business, which it readily admits is based on some pretty toxic, scary elements.

Dow's goals aren't just feel-good, they're actual, measurable, real-world targets. Boring percentages and dull financial metrics, and all this from a company that gave the world Agent Orange and the Bophal catastrophe. ExxonMobil's board couldn't get its major shareholders to approve one iota of real action to back up the outright lies of its corporate branding about the environment. Dow put its money where its mouth is.

And all they got for it was a glossy marketing campaign and imaginary brand value?

Equity, shmecklity, I say. Why the hell did Dow sign over its legitimate business strategy to the branding machinations of a bunch of communicators (internal marketers, and their external agencies)? What's a human element, anyway? The brand experts successfully abstracted a real company behavior, and then chose to communicate it in vague, feel-good, nonsense ways. Dow could have:

- Told the truth. A variety of communities, from the activists to the casually interested, would be interested in the specificity of Dow's commitment. These details, along with an honest and continuing description of the company's behaviors, should have been the substance of every social media interaction. Get people talking about specific facts, not somehow consuming branding dreck about a bike race around the world to support sustainable water.

- Been consistent. Goals, like life, are a process, not an outcome, and nobody needs to believe that Dow (or any company) will ever reach some ideal future state. So the 2015 goals are going to be out of date, or need to change (get better, faster, whatever); the company initiatives are real-time, so why wasn't the substance of its communications to involve its stakeholders in this ongoing evolution? Where's the global effort to write the goals for 2016?

- Challenged others to match its commitments. Greenwashing is a common shortcoming of most environmental programs, and the fact that marketers are left to deliver symbolic branding is why most people don't trust what the companies say. Dow was and is different; it has actually made business commitments, so why couldn't its outbound communications offer up standards to follow, examples for other companies to emulate, or even open source its activities so others could do them, too?

- Integrated its goals into departmental outreach. Ultimately, brands exist in corporate behaviors far beyond and apart from the creative inventions of marketers. Dow's sustainability goals must have had a significant impact on how those departments go about their business, so how were those actions communicated? How did they stand out from "regular" behaviors? How did Dow focus resources to understand how those actions would actually earn it more regard, inquiries and, ultimately, more business?

Instead, it gave the world the Human Element, only now it has to admit that the element is disposable. And the brand equity it built up via all that brilliant obfuscation?

Not terribly responsible, is it?

(39) Guns Don't Kill People

We hear this refrain every time a murder is committed, and it has helped weapons manufacturers and retailers duck culpability (well, the Second Amendment hasn't hurt, either). Does the same excuse work for all technologies?

I ask because a fellow dim bulber sent over a story about how the Iranian Gestapo uses an Internet monitoring system built by Nokia and Siemens to snoop on its citizenry. It is reminiscent in some respects to the revelation that Hitler used IBM systems to manage the Final Solution. In both examples, the allegation is that the technology providers knew, at least implicitly, that they were dealing with evil thugs, and that they may have had explicit knowledge that the deliverables of their contracts would get put to nefarious uses.

So the question is whether, or how much, should we hold these brands accountable when their handiwork enables their clients to do bad things?

I'm not sure I have the answer. There certainly was a flurry of angry tweets about Siemens and Nokia which, like most social media phenomena these days, peaked and subsided in about a nanosecond (a recent Twitter search yielded less than a dozen mentions over the past 6 hours, which is hardly a tidal wave). I can't find any proof that the IBM revelation in 2001 did anything to its sales. So we can argue about long-term damage to brand equity or corporate reputation, but the marketing industry is having a damned hard time finding any evidence of long-term benefits from heavy investments in and/or good news about brands.

Consumers are supposed to care about attributes associated with products and services, and then qualitatively weigh them when they make purchase decisions. Only they don't, at least not in anything past the immediate now.

I'm sure some IBM shareholders divested themselves of the stock when the Nazi connection first surfaced, and likewise more than a couple principled humans probably trashed their Nokia and Siemens phones. But after that initial rush to action, I suspect the relevance of the content receded into the blurry wash of Internet noise.

Whether we should care more is a deeper, more fascinating issue. Businesses often turn a blind eye to some of the potential negative implications of their behavior (complying with just the letter of the law on, say, product safety, or disclosing only the barest required information on company performance). Forget complaining about the health issues of eating sausage. We really don't want to see how it's made. Business is ugly: in a separate event, Siemens just settled with the World Bank for a cool $100 million to avoid conviction on charges of bribing government officials in at least 10 countries. Even in the most charitable analysis, it's worth discussing the indirect role companies play in influencing our lives, with at least some reasoned consideration of technology. Ultimately, guns *and* people kill people.

Social media give us the tools for such conversations, only I can't find much proof that they're being used that way. Instead, some folks declared that Nokia and Siemens are run by Satan, and others repeated the accusations. Some of the mainstream reporters added that the functions inherent in the Iranian systems are commonly used by other governments to accomplish less heinous goals.

And then Michael Jackson died. So much for the importance of context or continuity.

I don't think the Iran imbroglio will be enough to stop Siemens, Nokia, or any companies from writing future contracts that equipment could be repurposed to unexpected or just uncomfortable uses. Their marketing communications response has been (and likely will be) to say little to nothing.

To get businesses engaged in real conversation would take a real conversation among consumers and/or investors. Angry tweets are just light entertainment.

(40) Why Ads Aren't Enough

Did you know that a lot of oil tankers are floating just offshore from various refineries, filled to the brim with cheap oil, just waiting for prices to rise so they can get sold at a bigger profit?

That means less availability for shipping oil that's being sold and used now. More competition for tankers means they command higher prices, which in turn raises the prices charged to consumers and lead to...yup...higher prices for oil. Only then will those tankers start making port, just slowly enough to keep from literally flooding a market that has just gotten more lucrative again.

So tell me again what aspect of our addiction to oil is good for us?

- As the chief culprit behind global warming.
- With players ranging from Middle Eastern dictators and terrorists, to companies making more money than Midas could have ever touched.
- A pricing model based on the maximum amount of money that can be extracted from each step of the production and sales process, and experts committed to exacting said money.
- A consuming public (individuals and companies) that feels effectively stuck buying the stuff.

This isn't an industry with a chronic image problem: *it is a chronic problem*. The image is mostly accurate.

This puts its marketers in a difficult position, as oil companies are run by smart, principled people who see the situation, yet mistakenly believe that it can be best addressed by producing the worst sort of distracting, dishonest communications. Marketers and their agencies are all too willing to produce mainstream media advertising and digital campaigns claiming that the oil industry is actively working to get out of the oil business.

No it isn't, and it shouldn't have to pretend otherwise.

There are going to be billions upon billions made finding and selling oil 50+ years from now, and anyway, I couldn't name a single company that plans so far out (let alone commits to things for the back-half of this year). Too many people work in it, with it, or have some sort of dependency on it – from electronics companies whose widgets require power for those always-glowing red "on" buttons, to the folks who make plastic straws for McDonald's – for the oil business to disappear.

So why not tell the truth?

Oil and gas are what make vehicles run, heat and cool homes, and power the machines in factories that make all of the other things we buy and use (and many of the substances which those things themselves are made of). Only ExxonMobil, Chevron, BP, and its competitors around the world aren't in the "energy" or "solutions" business any more than Blockbuster provides "entertainment" (it rents DVDs) or Wal-Mart is in market for "aspirations" (it sells lower-priced good stuff). Oil companies aren't trying to fund wind-mills or harness wave-power, and they haven't dedicated more than .0001% of their budgets (or employee time) to anything "alternate."

Anybody who has an Internet connection and about a nanosecond of time to think about things knows this already.

It makes all the branding nonsense we see and hear about alternate energy seem so inauthentic, almost in dissonance to the near-constant reminders we get of the tangible reality of the oil business (like tankers waiting offshore to gouge us at the pump). Now would be the time for the companies to actually do things that matter: crazy, meaningful stuff, like dedicating some percentage of the price at the pump to alternate energy development...reach-ing out to customers to help (and reward) them for conservation...pass their own sustainable business operations plans, like the ones ExxonMobil recently defeated (resoundingly so).

Then they could talk about the reality of their business, not try to hide or distort it. Ads just aren't enough.

JUST FOR FUN: ETHICS ARE WORTHLESS

I've seen a few commentaries lately, suggesting that we need to rethink how ethics and social responsibility are taught in the nation's business schools... as the graduates of said programs are the leaders and operators responsible for turning our economy into a catastrophe. Opinions on the nature of business leadership frequently include mention of ethics, much in the same way that critics of medical education bemoan the lack of bedside manners among doctors.

As long as ethics are viewed as a voluntary market externality, we're never going to see enough ethical business practices to overcome the ever-present tendency for economies (and societies) to slide into amoral muck.

Why do we treat the actions that are supposedly most important to us as if they should be voluntary behaviors, or simply taken for granted?

Think about it for a minute. Laissez-faire capitalism is all about the pursuit of self-interest...building businesses might include other businesses losing said business, but that's the creative destruction that allocates money and influence to the actions of those who've been proven worthy by market relevance and success. If everyone tries their very best to invent and provide value, the marketplace will maximize business output, efficiency, and the quality of life for all involved.

What's the role for ethics? You have to choose to believe that there's some ultimate accounting of behaviors that rewards ethical actions – what's "right" is some good, un-cutthroat behavior, at some point – and moderate your actions accordingly. This invisible hand might involve the scrutiny of your consumers, critics, and/or a Higher Power, and it might defy every encouragement and indication you otherwise receive from the market.

And, as it turns out, sometimes it might forever defy experience, as some people really do get away with acting unethically. Or, conversely, something as nebulous as a user-generated definition of "ethics" means we all do at least some things that might be interpreted as unethical by at least someone else.

So ethics are as real as, well, as you choose to make them. Not a helpful business strategy.

Rules are meant to be followed. In any system or game, what's not explicitly forbidden is at least tacitly allowed, even if it's frowned upon or considered in bad taste. It's called doing what it takes to succeed. So when businesspeople follow their own narrow self-interest, like doctors who don't have much time for making nice-nice with patients, they're doing what they're supposed to do, according to the rules.

Further, we take ethics for granted, much like we used to approach the environment: they, like it, are just there, outside of the market, and a moderating influence insomuch as you might choose to dump your pollution there...or take cues therefrom for your business behavior. Its actual cost, or the cost of the risk inherent in depending on it, doesn't get expressed as real numbers in any equation.

So I wonder whether we should be mad a business leaders for doing what's expected of them? If we (investors, regulators, investors) expect something more, it should be articulated and, if it's important enough, required.

I think this is why I have such a problem with the CSR movement; it's just window dressing or, worse, like putting lipstick on a pig. Marketers let themselves get lulled into a false sense of relevance when management tasks them with making symbolic gestures in the name of ethical behavior.

It's not ethical anything. It's a lie.

Such actions should have dollar signs attached to them, so everyone can value them accordingly; if they truly matter, and are truly ethical, then people should be willing to pay for them. Otherwise, we're just talking about a market externality, and you can't depend on, nor can you truly value, ethical behavior.

And that's just worthless.

Chapter Five
Home Runs

Great branding and marketing happened all the time in 2009, only it often occurred in some less noticed and most unlikely places.

In fact, I'm not sure we possess the right criteria or language to agree on what "great" even means. So many things have changed – from our channels to our expectations – that much of what was celebrated in the media (and promptly resold to other clients) just left me flat. I had this sneaking suspicion that we were missing something all year long. A shared idea of purpose. Criteria for success. *A program.*

I wrote a number of essays on what I thought were home runs that you'd otherwise miss; when I reviewed them for this book, I discovered that they usually exhibited novel thinking in one or more of what I've concluded are the six categories, or "Six C's of Success," which are:

1. Channel. "New" shouldn't be a synonym for "digital" when it comes to media for reaching consumers. The truly inventive campaigns used new ways to communicate, like incorporating heaters in bus stops with ads, or newspapers that were written differently, not just reformatted to look like web pages.

2. Creativity. I'm a sucker for a good fart joke just like the next guy, but the really creative content in 2009 wasn't focused on making people laugh as much as inventing new ways to talk about products and services. Who would have ever thought of giving life insurance as a gift, for instance?

3. Competitiveness. Some marketers rejected the babble of talking about enhancements or selling imaginary benefits, and got back to talking about real differences with competing offers, going so far as to invent their own competition to crowd a market.

4. Content. Home run messages had meaning and relevance, not just entertainment value. One of the key winning ideas was to pull cam-

paigns back to the old-fashioned idea of sampling, which helped make a beer message very compelling.

5. Clarity. The best ideas weren't focused exclusively on marketing communications, but the business behind it. 2009 gave us examples of clients linking marketing efforts to results, which the media interpreted as punitive. It wasn't.

6. Call to Action. This was perhaps the most important quality of all. Home runs have objectively real actions attached to them, so they're memorable for what happened (and not for what people thought about them). So, for instance, an emotional attachment was less important than the offer to "try our toilet paper."

The Six C's cut across the more common criteria by which brand and marketing strategies are discussed; I think that one of the biggest risks we run is when we try to do "a digital campaign," or look at a business challenge in terms of the marketing tools available to us. Home runs go above and beyond those common vendor definitions, and are assembled by sometimes unlikely (or unexpected) elements.

They can also be nothing more than scrappy singles, to push the baseball analogy perhaps too far. I'm convinced that some of the best strategies in 2009 were mistaken for tactics; doing "little" things really well was perhaps one of the year's "big" ideas.

Here are 10 essays that illustrate putting some or all of the Six C's into action:

(41) Pledge, Or The Puppy Dies

Chicago Public Radio is approaching its latest fundraiser with an interesting twist: give now, and shorten the upcoming pledge drive.

I think it is brilliant marketing, for a couple of reasons:

- It targets active listeners, not samplers. The offer is irrelevant to folks just stopping by the station now and then, but to a regular listener, it's like promising to force some crazy relative to come live with you for a week. Saying it's irritating is an understatement; pledge drivers transform an otherwise interesting listening experience into torture. So the offer is immediately clear and relevant to someone who likes to tune in every day. No high concept, humor, or brilliant branding subterfuge required. Just pay up, or the puppy dies.

- It pitches giving without repeating the same pitch. OK, so if you're the type of listener who already gives annually to support Public Radio, you don't really need the pledge drive experience to get you to give again. You get it, even if you aren't required to pay for it. It's different for the freeloaders, though: all of the regular pitches to support Public Radio literally fall on deaf ears... *free* is free, and sometimes a compelling moral argument isn't so compelling. Threatening to disrupt programming for a week is lots more tangible. Forget the goodwill. Pay up, or tune out (for a week).

- There's timeliness to it. Don't just think about how good it would be if you made a donation, but do it now in order for it to help push off a day or more of pledge drive. This pitch comes across as far more genuine than the standard "offer only good today, or until when-ever." Pay up. Now.

Even better, the station is promoting a giving program called "High Fidelity" that enables ongoing, regular deductions from a credit card. So no annual renewal hurdles, and no regular intrusions into programming. Argu-ably, I bet a long-range what if plan is to migrate enough givers to such a never-ending subscription model that it might obviate entirely the need for pledge drives.

The sales pitch from any public media outlet is a tough one on a good day, right? It's like all of those "make a contribution" buttons on web sites... sure, it's worth fishing for the few who might give away money out of the goodness of their hearts, but with the many who might ignore the tug of those heartstrings are where the big dollars hide.

Asking for people to ante up for free media is kind of like putting a can with a coin slot in it on the corner, and asking folks to make a donation for the air they breathe.

Yet Chicago Public Radio has invented a compelling reason to give, made it stand out, and attached a timeliness to it, inventing some really, really smart marketing...sans complicated equations about conversations, viral transmis-sion, or other machinations of the modern and innovative.

It might make sense for some of the bigger brand names to tune in? Oh, and pledge some money while you're at it, or the puppy dies.

(42) Even Before the Ink Dries

Kodak has just announced its new "Print and Prosper" marketing campaign, and I think it's utterly brilliant marketing.

The premise is simple: Kodak printers use cheaper ink without sacrificing quality, so they cost less to use. As most everyone knows, at least viscerally, cartridges are the not-so-secret whammy that lets HP, Lexmark, Brother, and the other manufacturers push down the hardware cost...and then recoup everything, and more, through ink usage over time.

Gillette pioneered this approach with its blade pricing, though it has become so expertly copied that it risks becoming synonymous with hidden costs. Discovering the financial impact of using a printer is kind of like getting told that checking a second bag on an airline will be an additional expense... or that the car you think you just priced will cost extra thanks to various dealer fees. It just seems somewhat dishonest, even if the consumer should have consciously expected it.

So I like the Kodak strategy because it hits on a fact that requires no explanation, and declares that there will be no surprises. You don't need to deconstruct the message that Kodak printers are cheaper to operate. There's no hip imagery, music, or vain attempts to associate emotions with the business. Saving money is a happy emotion, and requires no elaboration.

This says lots about the authenticity of its brand, as well as its relevance. It's a welcome contrast to the nonsense feel good marketing on which it has been wasting its money for the past few years. People might actually buy the stuff because of this campaign. It's supported with an online calculator to figure out how much money you'd save (by asking details about the printer you're currently using, so it's also a nefarious swipe at gathering data), and there's a silly partnership with some "consumer advocate" to help expose the issue (it looks ersatz, and adds nothing). I'm sure we'll see the requisite Facebook page(s) and other social media expenditures that constitute the creative tax that agencies levy on clients these days.

I would have taken the plunge and added more operational components to it, like:

- Different pricing models. Cartridge purchases could be the basis of a loyalty program, allowing buyers to accrue value over time. Or how about a more visible spent unit return program that had some measurable deliverable that helped save the planet?

- Novel bundles. Why not put together a B&W cartridge and a supply of paper that it could cover? There's no good reason why ink and paper are sold separately, at least from a consumer perspective. Kodak could recommend the "right" paper for its bargain cartridges, and price the bundles (photo copying, color printing, etc.) to sell.

- New distribution. I'm thinking subscription here, or some other semi-automatic replenishment mechanism. There's also no good reason to make customers go to the store to buy cartridges, and usually it's because they've run out when they were trying to accomplish something (i.e. it's negative to the brand experience).

- Links to other divisions. Now that we can print more pages without guilt, couldn't Kodak offer an upload/online backup storage service (or, since the printed documents were already computer files, maybe the capacity to store and/or OCR hand-written edits, drawings, etc)? There must be a connection here to printing pictures.

- Long-term picture. A printer has the half-life of a flea, so it's effectively worthless by the time you've hooked it up to your computer. So why not sell subscriptions (or membership, or whatever) to them, instead of simply retailing stand-alone pieces of hardware? There could be a service component to such a relationship structure, too. So maybe people lease printers...then trade-in, trade-up, etc.?

The brilliance of Kodak's latest marketing is that it sets the stage for any of these possibilities...or for better ones, because it is simple, factual, and relevant. Win or lose, the company can aggressively improve and build on the campaign even before the ink dries.

(43) A Fascinating Experiment

Israeli newspaper *Haaretz* recently gave its reporters the day off, and had some of the nation's best authors and poets write the paper instead. Here's how the stock market report kicked off:

> "Everything's okay. Everything's like usual. Yesterday trading ended. Everything's okay. The economists went to their homes, the laundry is drying on the lines, dinners are waiting in place..."

A front-page story on a children's drug rehabilitation center ended with this:

> "I lay in bed and thought wondrously how, amid the alienation and indifference of the hard Israeli reality, such islands – stubborn little bubbles of care, tenderness and humanity – still exist."

I think it was a fascinating experiment, though I'm not sure what it was hoping to prove. Asking artists to determine what qualifies as newsworthy would seem to exclude other criteria, such as commercial or base entertainment appeal. Is that a good thing? Does it have any relevance to a potential future for newspapers?

It's certainly in stark contrast to, say, the Twitter feed, or any number of blogs that presume to provide content for the public square. One of the complaints against newspapers, along with any authoritarian provider of information, is that they presume to be authorities. There's something just wrong with a defined group of people defining what matters, or what things mean, just as there's something inherently right or fair about letting the crowd decide things.

So trading one group of elitists (reporters) for another (well-know artists) changes the content and tone, but not the structural imperfections of the medium, right?

Then again, abdicating control to the crowd is trading one authority for another, replacing our explicit awareness of the needs and limitations of traditional providers, for our implicit hopes that the crowd will be somehow better. It isn't necessarily more accurate, nor is it balanced, or particularly "just" in its randomness.

And it is rarely poetic. If social media are putting newspapers out of business (which I don't think is the case, necessarily), it isn't because the experience is an absolute improvement. It's just different. A newspaper written by artists is different, too. And my dim bulb conclusion is that the experiment does indeed suggest a future role for newspapers, whether delivered via print on paper, or electronic bits on screens.

The crowd can deliver immediacy and breadth, but has little to offer by way of analysis (relevance is a desperately subjective qualifier, and isn't a sum of frequency or virulence). The wash of content affectionately called ambient awareness isn't a replacement for meaning, it just redefines it as a pleasantly spun version of distraction. My bet is that people still thirst for:

- Facts that are objectively true (or at least we know why they claim to be so).

- Interpretation that is thoughtful (and we understand how it was arrived at).

The answer probably isn't to ask poets to write newspapers, however intriguing the product might be. Maybe there's a little side business here;

imagine a country's most popular artists in various media providing regular commentary of what they find most important in life. I'd read it, or watch it, or listen to it.

Haaretz explored a way to reaffirm the role of mediated content, and it was a brilliant idea. I wish more newspapers would quit the useless marketing and web-envy redesigns, and embark on similarly bold experiments.

(44) A Hot Idea

Kraft has put heaters in 10 bus shelters in Chicago to deliver experiential marketing for its Stove Top brand. I think it's a hot idea.

The premise behind the experiential approach is that branding needs to be brought to life, or dimensionalized through experience, in order to be memorable. It's a riff on the idea of sampling, only in this case consumers are getting a taste, whiff, or feeling that is relevant to a brand attribute, and not of a functional quality of a product or service.

This is about when the idea gets silly, of course.

When a corporate spokesperson says "Stove Top as a brand has a great equity in the area of warmth," it belies the mistaken belief that warmth can be owned by some thing called a brand. You see such words connected to other words in boxes on branding presentations, but the only place you find them in the real world is when you go and ask people what they think about a brand. Warmth could have appeared in a multiple choice list (a trick called "aided awareness").

But Stove Top is onto something: it's *doing* something.

Experiential marketing is a killer app for branding, not because it brings to life any esoteric pretensions of connecting otherwise unconnected attributes to stuff, but simply because it makes a connection. Consumers huddled in bus shelters will feel comfortably warm when they see the *Stove Top* ad. It would be just as effective as an air conditioner blowing cool air in the summer. Associating something pleasant with whatever it is that you're selling is a good thing. No words, nothing to deconstruct. On a cold day, warmth is a good thing. The medium is the message.

Science has proven that people remember things better when 1) they're happier, and 2) when there's multiple sensory support for it. We also know that there's no demonstrably reliable, causal link between good memories and subsequent purchase behavior, other than a broad "good awareness is generally better than bad, or non-awareness." So maybe experiential marketing is a chance for any brand name to use any sensory prompt, irrespective of whether or not it follows one of the dotted lines on a branding chart:

- Make check-out at the grocery faster.
- Slow down escalators when someone has trouble getting on.
- Ensure that taxi receipts more easily gotten, or readable.

Our modern lives are full of opportunities for small, beneficial improvements; change one, and attach your brand to the happier experience, and *voila*…it'll be remembered better than the most creative, cutting-edge commercial.

(45) Charmin Kicks Butt

Charmin makes toilet paper, and it has found a kick-butt way to deliver its brand to consumers: it opened a public bathroom in New York's Times Square, and invited everyone to, *er*, sample the product.

For anyone who has walked around New York, this is a big deal, as most restaurants make a point of barring you from using the facilities unless you're a customer. Hotels are a good shot, but they're not every block, and there's no guarantee they'll let you go. The Times Square area is a notoriously difficult place in which to find a bathroom, and yet it's usually jam-packed with tourists, day and night.

So in rolls Charmin with what amounts to a public service as much as a branding campaign.

Sure, it's a product sampling opportunity, too, only I'd imagine it's hard to compare toilet paper products without an actual bottom-by-bottom test. Charmin *works*, obviously, and maybe that's the only experiential attribute that matters when duty calls.

I'd suggest the *a-ha* of this campaign has nothing to do with wiping rear-ends, though.

Contextual relevance is one of the primary litmus tests by which human beings assign recognition, meaning, and importance. That means it changes based on lots of variables: who you are, where you are, what you're doing, what you just did, and what you are about to do next. And only the most broad or generic attributes are sustainable over time.

Think of how much time and money is spent trying to fine-tune branding messages. Little, if any, of it gets attached to brands in any meaningful way.

In this sense, I'd suggest that Charmin didn't have to provide an experience related to the attributes of its brand, functional or imaginary. It just had to do a good thing when and where people would recognize (and remember) it as such. The thematic relevance doesn't hurt, of course, but I wonder whether it's vital or even core to the execution?

Such a POV opens up a host of new opportunities for businesses to connect with consumers in real, meaningful ways. Who needs interruption or conversation when you can deliver a real benefit? That, my friend, is the bottom-line.

(46) I Love Luv Jozi

Cheap, imperfect product knock-offs are the bane of a branded products business, right? They pollute the value equation, and risk diluting the brand with ersatz materials, attributes, and associations. So why would a fashion brand create a knock-off brand on purpose? That's exactly what a South African T-shirt company called Love Jozi did...for two years, until it admitted to the ruse just before Christmas last year.

Luv Jozi (notice the purposeful misspelling?) was splayed on a range of cheap shirts supposedly manufactured in China (they weren't), then sold on a web site and promoted via a Facebook page. Also, the merchandise was actually distributed to flea markets and other city street vendors, just as you'd expect from a knock-off business. Bloggers ranted about the injustice, as consumers were made aware of the authenticity of the real Love Jozi brand.

It was alternate reality gaming meets culture-jamming, with a dose of irascible invention thrown in just for the hell of it.

Love Jozi took control of the inevitable knock-off viral meme, and by doing so strengthened the credibility of its brand value proposition. It gamed the system to generate publicity, and provided consumers with an indirect, but still real, way to interact with its brand. It didn't just fake an evil competitor...it created one, and the company sold real products to real people.

Was it disingenuous? Partly, I'd say, but I'm not sure I'm all that refreshed by the crude, obvious honesty of much of the viral nonsense that gets propagated into the ether these days (i.e. shouldn't I be more offended by the intentional time-wasting, society-sapping nature of the Burger King videos?).

I have a lot of respect for marketers who can see the marketplace in its totality, and devise programs that interact through and around it, and not just within it. Plus, it turns out that Love Jozi was planning to legitimize the knock-off as its own low-price sub-brand anyway, which is what prompted the disclosure late last year.

I wonder how many other knock-offs and social media trends are similarly contrived?

(47) Scarcity as a Benefit

Knob Creek bourbon has announced that it may run out of stock yet this summer, and that thirsty customers will have to wait until the next batch arrives on store shelves in November. I think this is brilliant, old-school marketing.

One of the most important brand attributes of successful products and services is *success*; consumers want to know that other consumers want stuff, and sales is a qualifier that goes far beyond conversation as proof of that interest. That's why movies strive for big opening weekends, and why a sellout of anything invariably leads to reservation lists.

While software mechanics strive to make supply meet demand in an idealized state of ongoing one-to-one perfection, a little extra demand goes a long way.

Think how many marketers fail to see this somewhat simple truism, and waste time and money trying to educate consumers about what they should know about stuff. The whole concept of differentiation relies on a series of attributes that are often lost on folks; consumers are supposed to discern the "bold" positioning of one product from the "reliable" qualities of another one (that are otherwise all but identical). This is especially evident in new product launches, which struggle to break through the cluttered mediaspace to get seen.

But who cares if a laundry detergent has 5% more stalagmites than another, or that one bottle of hooch is aged 9 years vs. 8? These can be very meaningful and relevant attributes, but the communications challenge is to make such things apparent in a nanosecond. Perhaps long-tail growth plans look smart on a spreadsheet, but I suspect that loads of people have lost their jobs before reality ever lived up to the aspirations of the far right-hand column.

That's why social media chatter isn't synonymous with sales, and why so many of the latest product campaigns have failed to deliver. Talk is cheap, if not outright worthless sometimes, and I think the definition of "success" in this business context requires the tangible, unequivocal truth of paid transactions. Anything else can be an enabler and/or sustainer, but not a substitute.

Which brings me back to Knob Creek. It announced that it is "letting its current supply run out," which "may" lead to shortages. It pretty much told its customers to go out and horde the stuff, which was great. It could have also applied some new media strategies to the ploy:

- Let customers register for updates/access to the next batch (even pre-order, though I bet there's some law against doing that online)

- How about a social media campaign letting drinkers post "their last Knob Creek experience" and enter some contest or game for a payoff via the next batch?

- Why not create a campaign that let would-be customers witness the production process? If it's the true differentiator, they've got the quickie notice communicated, so why not get folks involved in the education part? I could see an "Aging-cam" that let people stare at an oak cask. Nothing would happen. *Get it?*

Campaigns like this renew my faith in the marketing business. Scarcity is a brand benefit. I hope it's a successful strategy for Knob Creek.

(48) Insurance...Just What I Wanted!

New York Life has been running an ad campaign for a few months now, and I've got to say that the offer makes perfect sense...even if the premise doesn't, at least at first glance.

The idea is simple: give life insurance as a gift.

It fits right into the context of our lives today, just as the standard marketing themes of impulse, luxury, and wanton excess (in large or small servings) seem oddly detached. The premise that an insurance policy could be a gift is still a little strange – I immediately wonder whether giving someone a gift certificate for a flu shot would also qualify – but the more I think about it, the more it makes sense.

Tough times require thoughtful, responsible decisions in the place of what were once impulsive or frivolous choices. Responsibility, maturity, and the values those qualities both offer and represent are far more likely to survive the test of budget consideration, even if they don't quite fit the tweet-test of immediate relevancy:

"What did you get your husband for your first wedding anniversary?"

"I insured his life."

"Wow, you hopeless romantic, you!"

I find this campaign somewhat similar to the spots *Lexus* has been running for a few years now, in which a spouse wakes up on Christmas morning to discover in the driveway a shiny new luxury SUV with a big red bow on it. It's a nutty proposition, but innovating new uses for existing products is a powerful idea. In a challenging marketplace, no brand can afford to waste creativity on trying to attach abstractions to products or services, but rather finding ways to make stuff relevant to the lives of the people who are supposed to buy it. Consumers aren't asking for more Facebook friends or funny videos; they want to know if they can repurpose their toothpaste as caulk for bathroom tiles, or if company management really and truly knows how safe/risky a financial instrument might be. Marketers can run imaginatively brilliant campaigns declaring fossil fuels companies are leading the charge to green technology all day, but nobody will care until they see substantive and sustainable proof of said efforts.

So why not put a bow on a car, or wrap up an insurance policy for a birthday party?

Fitting what we're selling into the needs of consumers, instead of trying to make them need what we're selling, seems like a smart strategy these days. It doesn't have to be any less creative or sexy than the traditional approaches to market. It just has to be smarter. And more credible.

(49) I'll Bet On The People's Car

Tata Motors is going to auction its first 100,000 Nano automobiles in India to customers chosen by lottery, at a retail price that starts at about $2,000.

The thing looks like a Pinewood Derby body stuck on a lawnmower; it's named after an mp3 player; and it seems sized to fit four full-bodied Australopithecus, but nevermind all that: it's cheap, gets 55 miles to the gallon and travels about that far in an hour, and could forever change the automotive retailing landscape worldwide. It does so by two ways:

1. What it is. A small car made out of what might be no more than aluminum foil, mass-produced and sold for the cost of a really nice desktop computer, means that lots of people could buy it. So don't think about it as a second or third car...but rather just another car that could be used if and when useful. Suddenly, the debate isn't about replacement, but simply an alternative to driving one of those larger, gas-guzzling SUVs in the 5-car garage. It's very possible that the way to move the conversation about conservation significantly forward is to stop trying to have our proverbial cake, and eating it too. The Nano could get into enough hands to be a default choice when travel doesn't require great speed, style, or comfort.

2. How it's sold. A lottery is such a cool idea. It's a game, sort of, and it acknowledges demand without overtly trying to exploit it. The distribution challenge for the Nano is to get a lot of them out on the road as soon as possible; only then will people be able to get over some of their safety concerns (the presumption, however faulty, that big cars are somehow safer has helped drive the SUV business). I wonder it Tata will consider other sales models. I've got one idea: give the cars away, and charge for brokered fuel deals, services, etc. I suspect that this little vehicle has the potential to turn the auto dealer model on its head (pulling the model out of the grave first, of course).

I've been a fan of Tata for some time now. This is the company that bought Jaguar and Land Rover from Ford, both because it wanted high-end offerings, but also to repurpose the design and manufacturing knowledge across all of its product lines. Tata innovates, in real and meaningful ways, and isn't afraid to experiment with similar conviction. It's no surprise that it's selling Nanos by lottery; just like in the beer business, we're seeing some of the boldest, most radical marketing ideas coming from companies that don't come from the staid economies of North America, Europe, or Asia.

A true people's car like the Nano could really shake up our automotive markets. Too bad its estimated U.S. intro is two years away. I say let's skip trying to bailout or legislatively run the car companies currently in trouble – and evidencing no real capacity for risk or experimentation – and throw the public money to incentivize better competitors, like Tata, to move up their production plans. Why pay companies to try to come up with vehicles as competitive as the Nano, or to try and learn novel marketing techniques that Tata has already pioneered?

Let's invest in making a thriving market out of the crumbled dust of one that is terminally decrepit. Such a re-energized market could then decide which companies will ultimately win or lose. I'll bet on the people's car.

(50) I'll Toast AB

So Anheuser-Busch has come up with a new approach to compensating its marketing agencies, and the trade headlines say it "...whacks retainers..." as a casualty of the InBev-directed strategy to put the screws to said partners (oh, and trim $1.5 billion in costs that need to get trimmed).

I say let's toast Anheuser-Busch.

The old set-up let projects slide and change, perhaps even due to legitimate issues sometimes, which then let agencies add hours to their monthly retainers. It seems that A-B also regularly reimbursed certain costs that may have included agency charges or mark-ups.

Now, agency compensation will be tied to specific projects, with specific deliverables and due dates, and explicit front-end declaration of costs. Agencies, and their client, will have to live and die based on how strategic and smart they can be about the branding and marketing tasks before them. Those bastards at A-B!

The easy interpretation is to see this as an efficiency move, having nothing to do with the efficacy of marketing (or, worse, damaging it, whatever it is). But I'd like to suggest that it's *all* about doing better marketing, and that's good news for advertising agencies, and any other vendors who chase that sort of work. Here's why:

- The project approach better pairs costs with expected returns. The digital revolution has transformed what was once the ongoing, analog wash of communications into the quanta of Internet search and online campaigns, so much of the marketing work was getting "product-ized" anyway. Looking at an expenditure, and matching it with an expected outcome (whether sales, or some enabling other behaviors), benefits both parties in the deal: agencies can't bill wantonly, and the client can't blindly add revisions. Limiting scope-creep helps everyone, not to mention enabling better work output.

- It orients everyone on same outcome, not competing purposes. A big, still-unresolved bugaboo for the ad business in general is that many agencies think their job is to create great advertising. That's wrong: *they're supposed to help their clients sell stuff*, and advertising is one of many tools to help accomplish that goal. Imagine if the stated objective of a project were "to win an award at Cannes?" It sure would make everyone deal with it, up front. I suspect that the outcomes that'll drive most projects for A-B will have little to do with qualitative praise from the industry (or media), and lots to do with generating consumer behaviors. Again, welcome to the late 20th Century already.

- The focus stays on deliverables. Retainers are based on a process approach to financing, while project budgets are focused on deliverables. The criteria for any budget decision (or change) in the physical world's supply chain are based on the impact on outcome, quality, speed, etc. Most marketing agencies are rewarded for qualitative values – i.e. likability, retention, and lots of the nonsense metrics that get applied to the stuff they produce – versus the objective reality of their output. Projects mean a focus on making things happen in the real world. It could be carte blanche for hating your agency (or your client), and yet still loving your collaborative results. One more time, welcome to how the rest of the business is run.

- Perhaps last, though not least, cooperative updates to client-vendor relationships, as a general rule, are better than the surprise changes, which usually amount to the former firing the latter. No client is going to cut budgets they feel are beneficial to the company's bottom-line, so a whack at A-B's agencies means that A-B thinks there was some fat to be cut. Bone? *Naw*, probably nowhere near, and the brand isn't anything physical anyway. If it's a problem, where's the learned epistle from an agency exec defending the retainer, cost-overrun, *Mad Men*-era model?

Tell us how the former arrangement helped A-B sell any beer. In contrast, that's exactly what the new deal might just do. I say let's toast Anheuser-Busch.

Just For Fun: The Night After Christmas

'Twas the night after Christmas, when all through the store

Every employee was working at an annual chore:

The sale signs were hung by the windows aplenty,

In hopes that tomorrow, the store wouldn't be empty.

The merchandise all piled on every surface,

Hung on hangers, and displayed for one purpose:

For all the branding consumers weren't enticed,

The market requires the products repriced.

When out on the parking lot arose such a clatter,

One of the employees sprang to see what was the matter.

Away to the door, she flew like a flash,

Happy to stop bemoaning the store's lack of cash.

The moon glow on the pavement proved,

As illuminating as a video on YouTube.

When, what to her inquiring eyes should appear,

But the branding guru, and in his eye, a tear?

The marketing had failed, the sales not triumphant,

The guy sneaking away was the company's consultant.

More rapid than eagles his course was quite plain,

A getaway with successful branding he would claim.

"Now Viral, now Social, now Awareness and Retention!

On, Creative! On, Catchy! On seeking only mention!

The brand was made memorable, I won't take the fall!

Didn't they know it wasn't supposed to sell at all?"

As the store was chocked full with images and colors,

Assumed to have uses by exploited dullards.

On TV and online the ads, they still flew,

But there wasn't much of anything they'd do.

And then, in a twinkling, she heard only silence,

No customers, no visitors, no interested clients.

Turning around, she surveyed a store haunted by vague hopes,

As the branding guru seemed to say "adios, you dopes!"

He was dressed all in black, from his head to his shoes,

His clothes stylishly modern, a necktie refused.

A messenger bag of work samples flung on his back,

She could tell by his eyes that he'd never come back.

Armed with examples of what branding can do,

Off to find other clients' budgets to burn through.

Supported by metrics claims so esoteric,

Unquestionable, the canon of a Branding Church cleric.

So what if consumers didn't show they cared?

Paying for the brand attributes they weren't prepared.

Ev'ry abstract claim, all that clever stuff,

To prompt purchase behavior, it just wasn't enough.

And at stores like this one, left high and dry,

With very few options left to try.

No time for more hype, people don't buy air,

Expecting them to magically arrive is unfair.

So a righting of wrongs, a balancing occurs,

The process of matching wants and needs endures.

Give consumers real reasons for them to buy,

And sales results may warrant more than a sigh.

The staffer returned to repricing merchandise,

Ignoring the branding blather, to be precise.

Then the guru added, as if to her labor regale:

"Happy Christmas to all, and good luck with the sale!"

Chapter Six
What's Really Going On?

The short answer is that I have no idea. Nobody else knows, either.

Sure, there are a lot of theories, and you can't pick up a magazine that doesn't claim to list what happened in 2009 (and what you're supposed to do about it next year). There were even more stories during the year, created in the heat of the battles – or while folks were stumbling through the tall weeds, to be less militaristic about things – that aspired to provide some perspective. You probably sat through a presentation from a vendor, a trade show speech, or perhaps gave either or both yourself, always hoping to draw conclusions, and thereby give shape and reason to the chaos of what was going on.

Still, I don't think we know, and I worry sometimes that our need for answers sometimes keeps us from asking the right questions.

That's why most of my Dim Bulb posts were ultimately about the same thing: *what program?* Periodically during the year, I wrote about some possibility or trend that I suspected might be worth thinking about. I rarely had an answer, but I wanted to explore the possibility of different, better questions.

So, while everyone was writing about the miracle of social media, I asked about what happens to *trust* and other externalities on which communications depend. Ditto for a counterpoint to the growth in crowdsourced fact, when I asked about its effect on *objective truth*. While most experts agreed on what was important to consider, I looked in other directions, and:

- Contemplated the broader questions raised when companies selected to stop giving profit forecasts.

- Wondered about the impact of presuming that "free" is really the new model for making money.

- Pondered if the use of dubbed movie clips could be a new form of language in social media.

- Got all confused about the purpose of "mainstream" media, if it only reports on itself.

Ultimately, I don't think great prognostication is about being "right" or "wrong," but rather what insights and actions the process of prognosticating allows. It's unlikely that you can make a safe bet on one POV over another, however brilliant the observations appear at the time. It's especially troublesome when experts agree (what's most obvious to the greatest number of them is often the result of a particularly confusing battle, or the height of those weeds). Whatever answers you are given, it's probably more important to come up with more questions. And then repeat.

Here are some thoughts about deciphering what's up:

1. Consider there to be an inverse ratio relationship between certitude and reliability; what's most obvious now is probably going to be something we laugh about in a few years. Be a critical observer.

2. Language matters. When an expert or vendor describes a trend or case, make sure you all explicitly agree on definitions. One person's "success" is another's "irrelevance."

3. Look to areas that shouldn't be touched by an activity or trend, and see if you can find an impact (even indirectly). I'm convinced that many of the impacts of 2009 will emerge in places we least expected them.

4. Look to the past. No matter how new or futuristic something appears, it has probably happened before in one way, shape, or form. Conversational media is *not* rewriting the rules of civilization, for instance. Check out what other people did when faced with the same things we are.

5. Make sure you don't insert our present age biases into the past. 19th Century American Presidents didn't tweet, and the ancient Egyptians didn't care about brands. Try to see the Past for what it was, not what you want it to have been.

6. Technology is *not* agnostic; it changes the way we behave, even if it doesn't necessarily touch our underlying humanity. Multimedia is not just a tool, but rather a language that changes the *what* we communicate, not just the *how*.

7. Accountability all but evaporated in 2009, whether personal or institutional. With a tool like the Internet literally keeping track of everything that's said or done in the world, the most common trait it enabled was for everyone to "stick to their story" in spite of explicit

evidence they were wrong, or at least incomplete. This raises weird challenges for you, and I don't know the right answers.

8. Try to incorporate *behavior* into any trend; consider what people do, why they do it, and how likely they're going to do whatever it was sometime in the future. Take *no action* for granted. *Awareness* is not a synonym for *results*.

9. Patch together multiple trends, or POVs on the world, into your own customized observations. The gurus on social media really need to correlate their observations with, say, behavioral psychologists, or cultural historians. You think that'll ever happen on its own?

10. Aggressively conduct scenario experiments. Instead of taking the most popular observations about 2009 at face value, pluck out a key observation and play it out over time. If it's true, what will happen next? Why? How often? My gut tells me that much of what you'll be told about the year won't really tell you much about it whatsoever.

Here are 10 essays on some cross-functional, broad themes that might deserve a few more questions from you and your team:

(51) What Would Hitler Say?

Did you see the scene from the German movie *Downfall*, in which Hitler is re-dubbed to rant about Facebook's acquisition of Friendfeed? It's hilarious, and it's but a taste of the vast *Hitler-as-angry-mouthpiece* oeuvre. The mash-ups go back to early 2007 (at least), and the same clip seems to have been repurposed dozens, if not hundreds of times. It has been used to talk about:

- Michael Jackson's death
- The real estate crisis
- John McCain's election loss
- The new *Star Trek* movie
- Problems with Xbox Live accounts
- The Bills sign Terrell Owens

What's going on? I say it's description-by-proxy. Outsourced reaction. *Socialized evidence*, almost as if there's an emotional (or at least circumstantial) truth embedded in the clip of Hitler's tirade that's so generically relevant that it can be applied to any number of subjects.

"So-and-so really pisses me off, so don't take my word for it...here's a third-party description of how I feel." If some topic prompts particularly strong outrage, for whatever reason, it warrants the Hitler treatment.

Of course, it's mostly intended to be funny, and I don't want to read too much into Hitler having a particular relevance, as much as explore the utility of a video clip showing a character going ballistic (while henchmen stand around nervously for select crowd reactions).

But since such mash-ups are becoming more common, I wonder if there's some visual shorthand evolving in the social space, allowing for individuals to express themselves more easily, graphically, and somewhat more bluntly than they'd be allowed to (or allow themselves to do) otherwise? Video clips can be rich in information, and allow for the collecting of other complex and nuanced thoughts and emotions. Further, clips collect additional information when repeatedly used, right?

It's certainly a lot more nuanced than some textual entry on a blog or chat that reads "u suk."

(52) Trust in the Digital Age

With Facebook's latest change to its service terms creating a bit of a row, I thought it would be a good excuse to think about the role of trust in this digital age of ours.

The Facebook policy revision is at once simple and stunningly gigantic: it now claims "perpetual worldwide license" to anything posted on the site. The rationale is that it cannot control what happens to the stuff people post – pictures, for instance, can get forwarded to other web sites, perhaps even sold – so it doesn't want to get involved in possibly messy legal wrangling.

"We wouldn't share your information in a way you wouldn't want," founder Jeff Zuckerberg wrote in a post which, I assume, would only be shared in the way he would want. In other words, *trust him*. Similarly, we're supposed to trust:

- Google (and Yahoo, and any other search company) that has access to intimate details of your online behavior: what search terms you enter, the links you click, while its email service trolls the content of what you send and receive.

- Most web sites you visit, which work hard to recognize you, and then track how long you stay, and what you look at most.

- Your ISP, as it monitors your actions from site to site, and applies measurements commensurate with its perspective.

Never before has some much intelligence, creativity, and technology been applied for the sole purpose of watching, collecting, remembering, and analyzing all of that information about you for a variety of purposes, many of which will make it easier to manipulate you, some of which you've never even imagined, and a few that you'll never be asked to approve or refuse.

All in the spirit of technology making your experience better. Just trust it.

I'm convinced that if we swapped the words "secret police" for "technology services," lots of people would grab the nearest baseball bats and smash their computers to bits. Yank the broadband cable out of the wall. Throw the wireless modems out of windows.

Most of our ancestors lived in abject fear of such oversight. A seeming endless series of religious persecutions, totalitarian regimes, economic manipulations and forced emigrations taught them that trusting those in power is never, ever enough. It's actually pretty damn foolish.

So isn't it kind of weird that for all of the learned debate over ownership of digital assets (copyright for artists' work, for instance), there's been little disclosure or conversation about how much of everything else – everyday online behavior – is actually owned by the technology and service providers?

The big money-making of the digital age isn't distributing songs or photos for chump change, but manipulating and controlling this purchasing behavior, not to mention the overall access to knowledge and understanding, of zillions of consumers. Only nobody really talks about it in these terms. There's no public outcry for oversight, other than the Digerati blather following Zuckerberg's recent announcement.

We marketers depend on consumers having no issue with our intentions. Just click on the "approve" box, skipping all the mouseprint, and let's get back to surfing, chatting, or whatever. With that said, I know that Facebook doesn't have evil intentions, nor does Google, or any other company in the online services business. The only conspiracy here is that they want to make money, and that doing so will probably make our online lives somewhat easier and more rewarding. And, as of now, there's little consumer awareness of what (or how much) independence, anonymity, and ultimate control they'll give up to these businesses in the process.

Just trust that it'll all work out. And if that Facebook picture of me crushing a beer can against my forehead ends up getting bought by some company to feature on its web site, my only recourse will be to kick myself. Which is perhaps as things should be?

(53) Still No Free Lunch

Late last month, IAC Chairman Barry Diller said that it's "mythology" to view the Internet as a system of free communications. He's absolutely right; what's wrong is why he'd even have to say it, or that it would merit news coverage.

We're going to look back at this decade and laugh, if we're not too horrified by the inanity of our most popular business fantasies.

"Free" is one of the wacky theories that attempts to explain the ways the Internet is rewiring company and consumer interaction; its premise is that since anybody can produce and distribute digital content, the monetary value of writing, music, movies, and even conversation with one another, is just about zero. Money will emerge from other, perhaps ancillary sources to this content, mostly rumored to be advertising, only we already know that online ads don't necessarily do so well, generally, and that online consumers don't like seeing them, in particular.

The argument is just too intoxicating to ignore: since so many people are using online services like YouTube, Facebook, and Twitter, there'll be endless profits that'll inevitably come from all of that activity. The fact that these companies can't figure out how to deliver it – or can blithely claim to not care – is evidence of a temporary incompleteness of vision, if not an entirely new economic reality. Social media are rich with billions in unrealized value.

"Free" is actually worth lots. *Right.* Just like failing to find a price tag on an item at the grocery store means you can take it without paying. Our model for Internet commerce isn't a mathematical proof as much as a sketch for a perpetual motion machine.

In fact, I'd suggest the "free" model is better labeled the "stupidity" model, here's why we keep getting told about it:

- Consumers have to be dumb enough to miss valuing their own attention and time.

- There must be infinite resources of free stuff on which folks will spend their time.

- People with vested interests in promoting points 1 &2 get to tell us what it all means.

Diller, and other media moguls like Rupert Murdoch and Robert Iger, has a vested interest in challenging this model, of course, but his aspirations can be held accountable to, well, *accounting*. You don't have to throw away the basics of economic theory or human behavior in order to perceive potential profits, or rely on VCs getting investors to suspend their disbelief in order to realize them.

There are cataclysmic changes underway in the marketplace, and entire industries are reinventing their businesses in order to survive (while new ones are being created). But this change challenges us to see through or beyond the immediacy of the moment, and discern what's really going on.

Revealing the myth of "free" Internet business shouldn't be such a contrarian idea. In doing so, Diller affirms a deeper, more sustainable idea: there's still no such thing as a free lunch.

(54) The Revolution Will Be Fetishized

Now that the refrains of "Twitter Revolution" and "the first uprising powered by social media" are fading into the distant memory that is 24 hours ago, we can start debating what impact, if any, it had (or is still having) on events in Iran.

Social movements are, well, *social*, by their very definition; people have been agitating and acting together since the platform tools to do so were quill pens, inkwells, and whispering in one another's ears. Nothing new there. So the first question to ask is whether new media changed the conduct or outcomes of the social event itself (i.e. in Iran).

I'm not sure it did. Residents of Tehran used technology to make one another aware of the protests that emerged last week, but the activities were hardly oblique secrets. If there was a flashmob component to the marches, it was an extension of what could have been accomplished by other communications means; faster, perhaps, but not fundamentally different.

Did real-time posts convince otherwise disinterested people to get involved? Perhaps. Will it have made a long-term impact on perceptions and beliefs among non-participants? Very possibly. But again, these are impacts that could be achieved by any communications medium. There's nothing interactive or social about it.

It's interesting that despite the use of social media, copycat protests didn't immediately emerge in other Iranian cities. There's no way of assessing that as a failure of social media, the success of the government's clampdown on it, or the simple fact that interest in political disobedience was limited to the folks in Tehran. Those ex-Tehran protests started over the weekend, and could have been prompted by messages carried by donkey.

The thought-experiment riffs on the above are really intriguing, but I'm not sure they reveal anything. So what if George Washington's troops had tweeted about their suffering at Valley Forge, or the Mensheviks had similarly described the cruelty of their Bolshevik brethren. Would subsequent events have turned out differently?

Such analogies are less illustrative tool, and more unanswerable question; there are lots of variables that separate "awareness" from "behavior," and the latest figures on social media usage suggest that the vast majority of people tend to like to watch, not act.

Now, what about the impact social media have had on everyone else's experience?

This is a tougher issue to deconstruct. We all saw the unmediated content of the protests as it was recorded at ground zero, but what did we learn? Without context, they were just snippets from a narrative that escaped us. The "voices" we heard from were qualified by their desire to be heard, and not any other authority; we got first-person opinion, not anything even close to first-hand reporting.

In fact, social media didn't tell as much as it prompted interpretation; what little we learned directly originated in immediacy, and didn't necessarily lead to understanding. We know no more today than we did when the crisis started. We've just known less *quickly*.

And then there's the question of what we've done with that information. Not much, from as far as I can tell. Our participation, as spectators of events in Iran, amounts to a lot of *tsk-tsking*. Have people patched together imagery, or timelines, or otherwise assembled the bits of information into coherent pictures (literally and figuratively)? Did that information get shared with the folks back in Tehran in truly social give-and-take?

Or is the big idea that we can color our Twitter profile pics green, to better show our support to ourselves, as we watch the show?

If there's something really meaningful going on via social media right now, other than people trying to avoid the very real efforts of a very dangerous totalitarian theocracy that doesn't want its victims tweeting anybody, I want to know.

Ultimately, I'm an optimist, and I hope that social media would make more of a difference. Imagine if we'd had real-time tweets of ethnic cleansing in African or the Balkans, or abductees in our nation's rendition program could narrate their capture and transport? People might actually demand investigations, if not outright action. Or would they? Again, these tidbits of fact are no secret, and have been shared via blogs, web sites, snail mail, and printed agendas for major global meetings.

Here's one for you: what if it were Florida in 2000? A candidate wins the popular vote (vs. the Iranian pretender losing by 20 million or so), and then a court made up of unelected lifers decides that the *other* guy won. I wonder if there'd been tweets of the protesters there would have been more protests... or a greater popular uprising?

We can get thrilled about the events in Iran being a social media phenomenon, but they weren't. They were, and are, a reality phenomenon, and waxing poetic on the communications aspect of its description takes away from what's really happened (or not happened). It could be a minor blip in the history that dictatorship, or a country-changing event.

Social media won't be responsible for either outcome.

(55) All Bets Are Off

SAP and BMW have recently announced that they can't forecast what'll happen to their sales or earnings in the last two months of 2008, rendering 2009 as nothing more than a blank cell on their spreadsheets.

Isn't this the corporate corollary of saying the dog ate my homework?

Assessing current trends and then correlating them with past experience is very much a science, with only a pinch of estimation and/or "what if" thrown in. Some techniques are called "demand forecasting," while others are just a component of what businesses do: at a minimum, you need some context into which to place your inventory levels, prices, staffing requirements, etc.

Or maybe not. It seems that SAP and BMW are saying that the economic conditions are so unique, and so uniquely volatile, that no such context is visible. All bets are off.

It's a frightening prospect, if you think about it too much. What they're effectively saying is that nothing they have ever said about the power of their brands is true. There is no reliable consumer preference, and they have no understanding or expectation of their outbound marketing or sales efforts having any dependable effect. There's no ultimate payoff from those massive expenditures they explained away as "investments in brand equity."

Their brands, and businesses overall, at powerless against the vicissitudes of the marketplace.

We saw a related move by many big-name retailers earlier this year, when they backed away from the tradition of reporting same-store sales each month (also called "comp sales"). While this activity was a great insight into the ongoing performance of the businesses, management claimed that it was just the opposite.

It turns out that, while brands perform over time...*how much time* depends on how long of a period you want to measure. Whatever it is, the brand requires more, therefore you can't hold it accountable during whatever stretch you considered. It needs at least a day more, so all bets are off.

If brand marketing can't be relied upon to deliver any reliable results, maybe it would make sense to pick a number anyway. Make it terrifically conservative, or some permutation just shy of selling nothing at all. The lack of information isn't left blank or open in the minds of consumers or stock analysts; no information is the same as bad or negative information, so the businesses get whacked anyway. And I also wonder how they're planning marketing going forward. If nothing offers any indication that it'll work, what components get added to the go-forward budget?

Since all bets are off, perhaps it's time to experiment with radically new approaches to marketing?

(56) HAL Did It

Yesterday's report on the causes of the crash of Air France Flight 447 is incomplete, and the reliability of the investigation's findings will never be without question. But the broad conclusion is probably all-too true: the computer had something to do with it.

Well, it's more than likely that many automated systems played roles in the accident, but it seems to have started with the plane's speed sensors yielding incoherent readings. The bad data may have tricked other systems in doing things that weren't in the best interests of staying aloft. Analysis of the wreckage suggests that the pilots tried to land the plane on the water, as if they'd eventually wrested control from the computers, only too late.

Automation is a wonderful and frightening aspect of our lives, isn't it? From toasters to power steering, we rely on machines to do things that our ancestors either had to do manually, or couldn't do at all. Computers have made that automation much more pervasive: we expect our hard drives to preserve our family pictures, just as engineers at nuclear power reactors depend on software programs to make sure the fuel rods don't overheat.

I'm a firm believer in habit and routines as powerful brand attributes, and computerized automation is a key strategy for delivering it. Subscriptions, 1-click purchasing, product suggestions based on past interests, and automatic upgrades/renewals are as important as any conscious attachment to a product or service, perhaps even more so. From a functional perspective, "smart" devices can outperform "dumb" ones, generally, which means they can charge more for delivering better experiences.

Only now I'm becoming more aware of the downside to relying on something unconsciously, and it's called *dependence*. An automated function requires an abrogation of authority, or power, from beneficiary to provider. Because the platform on which I type this essay has all of the editing functions represented as buttons, I've never had to learn how to program in HTML. I rely on cruise control in my car to keep my speed constant, instead of learning to do with foot and pedal. Forget to send me the subscription renewal, and I might neglect to prompt it myself.

And when the pitot probes fail, the plane is sent into a literal tailspin.

We're not always aware how much we give up more in order to get more from our automated devices and services; making automation smarter, or more pervasive, doesn't necessarily mean it's any more *reliable*. Greater responsibilities increase the range of possible failures. Even if machines achieved consciousness, they'd still be prone to making the same mistakes in judgment that we make, wouldn't they, or it, or whatever?

God forbid machines developed attitude, like HAL9000 did in *2001: A Space Odyssey*.

This condition in our lives is what fuels some of the interest in the Maker movement; their premise is that we'll find greater fulfillment from our lives by taking active control of them. That means making stuff instead of outsourcing it to someone or something else. I wonder if events like the Air France crash (or any of the lesser, daily instances of automated things failing to perform) will get people thinking about the trade-offs they make in their lives between control and benefit?

- Could a next high-tech gizmo purposefully put more user controls back into users' hands?

- Maybe a subscription service could solicit more engagement, more often?

- Imagine automatic monitors, sensors, or services that required active, conscious involvement from operators, not less?

At least when it comes to critical stuff, like managing ICBMs or flying airplanes, maybe we don't want HAL to be able to do it?

(57) John Quincy Adams Didn't Tweet

The Massachusetts Historical Society is publishing the one-liner diary entries that President John Quincy Adams made in late August, 1809; his posts were all 140 characters or less, so it's doing it via Twitter. You can read them as if he's tweeting each day, 200 years later.

Adams has 4,200+ followers, so a few social media advocates have said this proves there's value in micro-blog (short) posts. While the technology of Twitter may be new, the desire and utility behind the behavior is hundreds of years old. If Adams could tweet before there were electric lights, shouldn't we all consider it almost an obligation to do so now?

No, but the real history behind it is pretty interesting:

- Diaries humanize experience. Adams described August 6, 1809 like this: "Thick fog. Scanty Wind – On George's Bank. Lat: 42–34. Read Massillon's Careme Sermons 2 & 3. Ladies &c. Sick." *How cool is that?* It's like you're there, standing in a long ago moment that otherwise evaporated the moment after it was immortalized.

- The brevity of the entries isn't a plus. Adams kept other, more detailed diaries, so it seems that his log was more of a table of contents, or memory prompt. For all that I think I get from reading it, the entries were cues to lots more that only Adams could recall.

- At the time, nobody would have cared anyway. Back in the dark days of Analog Existence, knowing what others were doing or thinking was based on infrequent input, and lots of assumption. Adams' fellows wouldn't have felt the need for the incessant quanta and abbreviated detail of tweets.

- Everybody kept lists...for themselves. Thomas Jefferson recorded every bottle of wine he drank for a quarter century (and how much he paid for each). Emily Dickinson wrote poems for herself. The centuries-old tradition isn't to share this information, but rather to record it for one's own consumption.

Interestingly, Adams must have felt that he could capture what was important to memorialize in a single entry each day. So he wasn't a "proto-tweeter" by any stretch of the imagination.

There's nothing ambient, or constant, or social about keeping a diary. Tweets are disposable, life histories are not. We are frail, impermanent human beings, and we have a natural desire to want to capture some small part of our brief time on this planet. That's what Adams did.

It's not different from what you or I could do. Typed. In pen and ink, or even using a crayon. Capturing tidbits of existence that will help give shape and form to our memories down the road. Noting things that matter, presuming the only person who will ever want to read them again will be ourselves.

In that sense, the former President was a lot like us.

(58) Individuals and Crowds

The last year's worth of financial news nonsense has got me thinking again about the divergent roles individuals and groups play in our lives. I'm torn between what, or whom, I'm supposed to trust: it seems like the broader and robust my access to the world gets, the less I know or believe. I rely more on what is immediate and personal, and the things that I know are true get simpler and basic...just as the credibility of larger, more complicated subjects becomes hazy and elusive.

All of us might live in a networked, ubiquitous net of information, wherein communication is as instantaneous as it's incomplete, but we also live in ever-smaller, walled communities of knowledge, in which people still speak in complete sentences. I've got loads of Facebook "friends," but my friends on whom I rely for insight or counsel are a much smaller, tighter community, defined by lots of criteria that groups don't provide, let alone require.

I can't decide if I' a cranky Luddite, or one of disparate number of real-life Hari Seldons.

When it comes to financial news, was the authority of content simply a ruse of intermediated distribution? A quirk of technology history? Was it opinion elevated to the status of truth because we just didn't know better?

Between cable television and the blogosphere, we now know that there aren't just two sides to every story, but a limitless number of perspectives. So none of us have to agree on which version of reality we choose to believe; in fact, because there are multiple versions available to us, we can pick one, and then organize (limit) our subsequent content consumption to support that choice. Or we can entertain a few simultaneously, reminded that an understanding of reality is never more than an opinion, and not a reflection of fact.

Can we crowdsource truth? I know there have been lots written about it, and companies are spending mucho dollars betting that throwing marketing content into various online services will result in consumers separating fact from fiction. I'm certain we can crowdsource cynicism, disbelief, and impatience. And I know crowds tend to move people to harden their positions and beliefs, so a lot of social media is less revelatory, and more an echo-chamber for prior-held thoughts.

When I think about individuals and crowds, I see that we're now living through our first *disintermediated economic crisis*. The Iraq war could have been our first geopolitical version, only battlefield reporting was/is tightly controlled, many of the would-be bloggers don't write in English, and lots of people don't really care about something unless it impacts them directly (a la a loved one in the conflict, or in the case of the economy, less money in a 401(k) plan).

And guess what? For all of our access to information, we're getting no real insight or certitude from the crowd, and I bet if you're like me, you're turning to people in your immediate sphere of experience (real-world family and friends) for information. It's funny that so many calls are being made for more transparency in, say, how the TARP funds were spent, yet our problem isn't that we don't have enough information...it's that we don't have the tools to decipher, correlate, and complete all the information the crowd is giving us.

What a crappy time for traditional journalism to be evaporating, eh? As the roles of individuals and crowds continue to diverge within the mediasphere, knowledge is disappearing in the gap.

(59) Is Search the Anti-brand?

I wrote an entire chapter in my book, *Branding Only Works on Cattle*, about how the ubiquity of information available to consumers via Internet search (access, richness, and authenticity) would destroy the fundamental, command-and-control presumptions of branding. Thanks to a tip from a fellow dim bulber, today, now I'm thinking that maybe I got it backwards?

"Wouldn't it be nice if Google understood the meaning of your phrase rather than just the words in that phrase?" asked the company's CEO Eric Schmidt on an earnings call earlier this year. He was referencing a broader company mandate to use brands to help clean up the "Internet Cesspool" of content. A company update issued in mid-January purportedly made it easier to prompt branded content with search queries, all in the name of providing better relevance.

Do you want your mind read? I know why a brand would want to do it, which is why there's lots of money in it for Google if it can make it work:

- A good number of Internet searches don't involve brand names at all: people might look for information on a trend, topic, or thing that doesn't have a logo on it.

- For those searches that do involve brands, the intent may not to be to find any content that the owners of said brands provide.

- A good number of Internet queries, like questions in real life, aren't even fully formed: we human beings tends to ask about things without necessarily knowing what sort of answers we're looking for, if we're looking for them at all.

If, through a combination of secret codes, severed chicken feet, and large cash payments to Google, brands could get better teed-up to complete/answer those queries, all would be good again in the branding world. Forget trying to get consumers to attach qualities to brands through humor, repetition, and effort. The algorithms would do it.

I'm having a hard time reconciling this with my perhaps Utopian dream for Internet search.

In my crazy thinking, a truly consumer-driven search experience would rely far less on *guesstimating* the right answers, and helping people figure out how to ask better questions. Think about it: isn't it kinda strange that there's no how-to or FAQ for using Google (or any search engine, for that matter)? It's not like searching is so simple and obvious. We know that's not the case, as it's more than likely that you've not found what you were looking for in a recent search (or, if you've ever tried to explain how to use it to someone over the age of 60, you know that search is not intuitive at all).

So if there were better explanations, and then easy-to-follow rules for queries – like declarative sentences or questions, maybe requiring a single active verb, or providing categories of key page resources from which to choose (like commercial or not) – wouldn't people get better answers?

I'm a big fan of "vertical" and "social" search, only because they rely, by definition, on matching certain types of information with specific queries, like "best hotel room." They publish their ranking rules (usually); better yet, those searches don't rely on the technical or monetary resources of marketers, but rather tee-up the answers from the experiences of other proles like you and me. But those probably aren't the answers brands want us to find.

Greater minds than mine can probably explain this situation far better, though rarely do they choose to do it in plain English. So which is it: does Internet search give companies the ability to manage (i.e. control) the conversation about their brands, or is it the tool to uncover (i.e. free) reality in spite of said efforts?

It's most likely both, right?

(60) Value

Lately, I've been thinking a lot about the utility of ad placement on social media sites, and whether it's the most enlightened way to monetize services like Facebook or Twitter.

I'd posit that there are two broad and somewhat mutually-exclusive schools of thought on the subject: one looking forward, and the other back.

The "forward-looking" model is extremely hopeful, and suggests that online commerce occurs within self-contained ecosystems. Activities and pricing are determined by transparent communications and the other attributes of efficiency. These principles apply to all types of commercial communities, whether eBay or some proprietary site for sourcing industrial parts.

Participants will pay for the value they receive for access to these services, whether as buyers or sellers.

Interestingly, when applied to social media sites, it's assumed that the value to participants of their participation is zero, and that the cost of that participation to the operators of the sites is effectively free. People don't pay for chatting or trading funny links, as if the content is somehow an externality to the pricing model.

The forward-looking model suggests also that such content will always be value-less, and that profits will have to emerge from activities "around" it, like ad placement, sponsorships, and other ways of charging commercial interests for the privilege of accessing the folks doing all the free stuff.

I think this approach is distinctly old-fashioned, at least going back to the days of broadcast TV, when channels gave away content, and then charged advertisers for promoting before and after it. The only difference is that Facebook or YouTube are outsourcing the programming, and getting it for free. The efficiency of behavioral ad targeting is what makes it new. Didn't online portals do sort of the same thing a decade ago? We know how quickly those futuristic visions faded into past tense.

Which brings me to the other approach for understanding value in social media, which is "looking back"...not just back to the heyday of mass media, but really back, like many hundreds of years prior, to the model of the medieval marketplace.

Markets emerged (and thrived) before there was a thing called "legal tender" or anything even approaching a standard currency. People bartered merchandise, gossip, and traded their time for the very experience of participating in a local confab. They paid for the privilege, and got paid for it, only not in cash. Value was a quality of the participation itself. The monetization came later, and not always in the best interests of the markets themselves.

So you probably don't go to social sites to transact business or spend money, right. But *value* still drives every visit; you wouldn't go if it didn't. That value isn't an externality to the experience – at least not for the experiencers – but rather central to the purpose and function of the "social" market.

You do pay for your visits, and you get paid for visiting. Just not in cash.

I wonder if we could invent ways to better recognize and reflect this type of value, instead of taking it for granted? For instance:

- Could a sponsor offer a way to credential users, in a real and meaningful way (i.e. not just allowing them to anoint themselves as "power users"), that allowed for their voices to be better heard and appreciated?

- Could brands help visitors find meaningful sections or areas on sites, and somehow improve how content is shared?

- Imagine a loyalty program that awarded points for frequent visits, or if participants paid for admission, so to speak, because they received some added benefit from conversing with one another, or with a corporation?

We human beings have long believed that the most important things in life are, *only maybe there's no such thing as "free"* but, rather, just instances wherein we can't (or won't) assign and measure the real locations of value.

Ultimately, I suspect that the opportunity for social media is to do just that.

Just For Fun: Rewards Card, Step Two

How many "reward cards" do you have, or loyalty programs do you participate in?

When I think of a typical day, I can't think of a commercial transaction that doesn't come with a clerk or cashier who asks, "are you a member in our blah blah blah program?" Books. Office supplies. Gas. Pizza. Groceries.

I don't feel loyalty to any of them. At best, they're *why not programs* – as in why not get the discount, or get thrown the occasional bone – but my purchase behavior is far more dependent on convenience, selection, competitive pricing, service, and habit.

Most of my buying routines would be the same had the rewards programs never been invented. This is a field in dire need of a strategic step two.

Consider Dominick's, my local Safeway grocer. Using a "Fresh Values Card" trades minor discounts for the right to track my purchases (so they can use that data to make better stocking decisions, and proactively market to me). This quid pro quo doesn't make me feel anything in particular toward the brand, other than somewhat exploited.

Then come all of the cross-promotional deals: I can earn airline miles, contribute funds to a school, accrue money for college, and even get free gas. Again, there's nothing proprietary about any of these sales offers, and they're all dependent on me spending more at Dominick's. It's clear that they're also all but automatic, as various computer programs track and process my activity, and then spit out the required discount cards and codes

It makes me wonder about who is being loyal to whom? I prove my loyalty by buying ever-more things, and Dominick's shows its loyalty to me by giving me a discount, whether in the form of a price cut or cross-sales offer? That's not loyalty, it's commerce, plain and simple. I earned the discounts. There's absolutely nothing wrong with it, but it doesn't build or sustain anything. Dress it up with any permutation of technology platforms and third-party deals, and it's still sales promotional activity.

I'd imagine that the next step in loyalty/rewards strategy would be to find ways for company and consumer to do things that affirm and grow true loyalty. To that end, I have three ideas to consider:

1. Citizenship. Why doesn't my grocery store host local improvement projects in our community? Skip cutting deals with BP, and make one with the grade school down the street that needs new band uniforms. Not everybody would buy into the deal, but those that did would feel a lot more toward the store than gratitude for a slight price break. Why not make a restaurant frequent eater card contribute to the local food bank?

2. Consistency over time. Don't focus on size of basket or aggregate volume of purchases, but consider regularity of those transactions. Isn't a shopper who visits with some periodicity (a weekly visit, for instance) probably far more loyal than somebody who uses his card 3 times a year? There should be recognition of that former behavior, incentivizing the routine of visits – tell me the cabbage I love is on sale for the day I'm likely to visit, or update me that books by my favorite author just went on sale – instead of simply rewarding aggregate purchases. The benefits could accrue to the shopper, or to the community (see prior idea).

3. Consumer participation. Ultimately, the value of social media isn't going to be for ad placement or the swapping of inane lifestyle tidbits; rather, it lets the purchaser take part in the production process (and, in doing so, both improve it, as well as make it feel more personable and ownable...i.e. feel loyalty). Ask consumers to help with issues of food assortment, menu listings, operational questions, then reward their participation.

I have a feeling that the second step in rewards and loyalty strategy will not be based on buying, but on all of the behaviors that come before and after it. Selling will be a natural and regular outcome, not the key input to the equation. So, not to get too esoteric on you, but the equation will get *flipped:* companies will do things that prove their loyalty to consumers, and then consumers will reward that behavior with purchases.

Chapter Seven
The Experts Have Spoken

The importance of research was never more apparent than in 2009, so it's too bad that much of it was self-serving sales tripe.

I know it's partly a function of technology and culture, as it's cheap and easy to produce and distribute surveys, polls, white papers, studies, flowcharts, slide presentations, and the other marketing detritus that hopes to disguise function with form. If people aren't supposed to believe outright marketing communications anymore, maybe the occasional authoritative study can help, right? Skip telling people what you think, and instead tell them what *they* think.

And then sell them something. So in 2009:

- Social media experts presented research proving the surprise efficacy of social media.

- CMOs talked about "the transformative role of marketing across the enterprise" because that's what they're supposed to talk about.

- Digital marketer studies presented research arguing that more marketers should spend more money more often on digital marketing.

- Consultants who promote behavioral marketing produced studies to substantiate their POV.

The list is endless, actually.

I'm surprised more of it didn't get challenged. You'd think that financial reporters would be critical of, say, vague measures for brand value that claim to affect billions in stock prices, and then evaporate when the market tanks. Call out new media sages who claim that consumers have recently evolved into a new species, as a substitute for marketing that prompts old ideas like selling stuff. If you follow the money behind many of the studies offered up as agnostic truth, you soon discover that they're really the product of one commercial interest or another. There's nothing wrong with corporate-sponsored research, of course. But should we presume that there's *no* reason why such activities get funded?

And isn't there something fatally flawed about this approach of holding up a mirror to an audience, and then telling them what you saw? Where's the interpretation and extrapolation that would yield actual insights – even risk being wrong, or incomplete – so businesses could make more strategic decisions?

That's what I tried to do during the year in Dim Bulb essays. I've collected 10 of them, each trying to go beyond the obvious interpretations blessed by experts (or some services provider with a sales pitch). I ran into more questions than answers. So let the gurus speak of conclusions; here are the top ten themes I'd wonder more about in 2010:

1. We haven't found the missing consumers. While lots of research claims to prove that consumers have morphed into active users of social media, it turns out that a vast majority of the people who used to watch TV (or read newspapers) aren't creating blog posts or tweets. So what are they doing? Watching?

2. People are defaulting to trusting one another over all other sources of information. This has serious implications for how we communicate commercially (i.e. is getting a friend to tag an acquaintance the same thing as a reasoned referral or recommendation?).

3. CMOs are in trouble, if you believe research that claims that the vast majority of them are "happy" with their external agencies, and that two-thirds of them think the most important attribute for job applicants is that they're "creative."

4. fMRI could be quack science, claiming to measure how brains respond to brands when the truth is that there's no direct measure for how brands differ (other than in a metric much like "volume"), nor how those mental impulses were created or nurtured. Consider phrenology or telepathy as possible alternatives.

5. Social media need better measures than word tracking. While a number of tools exist to create pretty charts of online activity, they could amount to weather maps with no geography underneath (i.e. no connections to topics, issues, relevance, or ultimate sales purpose). The research suggests otherwise, which means you should be worried.

6. You're not an idiot or a Luddite if you haven't embraced social media with open arms. Much of the research is biased, self-reflective nonsense, in my humble opinion. Come up with a reason to do it...other

than a need to do it...and try to wrest some business benefit out of it.

7. Consumer behavior has changed beyond the impact of conversational technology and the economic meltdown. Some research suggests they're returning to their reliance on *experience* and direct relationships, which shouldn't be so surprising.

8. Sometime next year (or soon thereafter) you're going to have to decide how much performance information (historic and predictive) you choose to share with the outside world, particularly if you're a public company. The trend is to share less, so will there be an opportunity to differentiate your business by producing more?

9. Your measures of brand value are going to get more specific, tangible, and objectively real. There were far too many surveys in 2009 claiming to track the ups and downs of brands, which crashed like a car wreck into the reality of how the same brands were performing the marketplace of consumers buying them...or not.

10. The next year is going to reveal really strange, interesting things about social media, from usage numbers, to the revelations of just how much information they collect on their users (and this aggregation of data will likely be the way they try to make money). Think about these implications before you encourage your employees and/or customers to live on said media.

Here are the top essays that further explore new ways to interpret and question research:

(61) The Missing Consumers

While the mainstream press, and most digital marketing firms, are convinced that social media are changing the consciousness and habits of humanity, I've chanced upon two studies that suggest otherwise:

- Only 5% of blogs are updated more than once every 120 days, and less than a million are updated every day. Out of 133 million blogs included in the late 2008 survey by Technorati, most of them are abandoned after the first post or two.

- While blogging has subsided to levels last seen somewhere in 2005 or so, about half of Twitter's micro-bloggers post, or tweet, less than once every 74 days. Most of the platform's traffic is generated by 10% of its users, according to this Harvard study.

Those are still staggeringly large and directionally important numbers. Advocates and detractors will incessantly debate them, but I think the idea that more people will communicate with one another more often, and for more reasons, is all but a forgone conclusion. Bickering about the details doesn't change the inevitability of the future.

But the usage numbers do bring into question 1) when will that future arrive, and 2) how will we get there?

The perception that social media usage is today's cultural and communications phenomena has led many companies to invest in experimental programs, then struggle to invent ways to measure them. However creatively memorable the campaigns have been, the numbers mimic the ersatz measures for internal states of brand that never quite felt right in the old days (best case), or reveal clicks, time spent, or other metrics that would consider even indirect relevance to branding an accomplishment.

Now consider the possibility that the reason why the numbers don't add up is because people aren't using social media as much as we were led to believe?

Facebook registers a zillion clicks every nanosecond. So does YouTube. But visiting sites for entertainment or conversation isn't new; we've been doing it in analog reality since Ogg debuted his first finger painting on a cave wall in Lascaux. The big aha of the social web is the democratization of content, both creating and sharing it. The consumers to whom we want to sell have become producers, or so the liturgy goes, who insist on participating in our businesses. Blogging, of any sort, is a primary way they narrate and advocate that participation, and it's supposed to change the way we deliver branding.

It turns out that there are just far fewer of those consumers online at any given moment. Further, if there aren't so many of them actively doing anything, do we consider them "evangelists" spreading the word into the cosmos, or perhaps a small cadre of individuals who are busy effectively talking only to one another?

Here's the scariest thought: what if all those consumers who abandoned traditional media, and rejected the presumptions of marketing upon which we have for so long relied, are still missing?

(62) True Lies

A recent Nielsen study revealed that people most trust what their friends say about stuff, and that they trust generic online consumer opinions as much as they do branded communications.

I think this has more to do with the contextual reality of the expectations than it does with any inherent trustworthiness in a particular communications medium (or lack thereof).

Media are agnostic when it comes to meaning and utility, or so this dim bulb believes. TV isn't more or less authentic than the Internet, and information gathered from a chat room won't inherently prove more useful than the same info copied from a roadside billboard. What differentiates trustworthy content from that which is lesser so has everything to do with, well, *content –* i.e. what is being communicated – and the context in which it's being shared (i.e. the immediately obvious and beneficial use for the information).

As such, trust is based on expectations: if I know that TV ads are generally funny but reasonably devoid of motivating info, I'll trust them to perform to those low standards (a result borne out by another Nielsen study on advertising), so it's less distrust and more the absence of it altogether? If I usually associate texts on my phone with friends or other reasonably intimate info, and I get generic sales pitches instead, I'm going to learn to trust that channel to tell me nothing useful, too (also confirmed by the Nielsen research).

Conversely, if I were surprised by some consistent delivery of meaning and utility via TV spots, my trust would increase, as would my appreciation of mobile marketing if it similarly improved?

The Nielsen data seems to support such extrapolation: the most trusted "form of advertising" is a recommendation from a friend, which is something you'd expect to have merit coming from someone you know (or in response to a direct question); some of the lowest are online video and ads before movies, which are presented without regard to the who, what, where, when, or why of context. It doesn't help that the content is often purposely pointless.

Why do "branded websites" tie "consumer opinions posted online" for trustworthiness? Similar expectations: the corporation is going to throw blah blah at me, and the aggregate conclusions of the crowd are going to trend toward some common denominator. In both cases, we get what we pay for, so to speak.

It's marvelously intriguing information. Just think how many marketers are running away from traditional media, like newspapers or radio, because they think consumers don't trust them anymore? An equal number of them are racing to embrace social media campaigns because they are assumed to be more trustworthy. Both assumptions are wrong. Why don't we focus on making the conduct of our businesses meaningful and useful, and then structure the marketing communications to deliver that information?

(63) Survey Says...Uh Oh

A survey of top marketing executives at 180 businesses late last year revealed lots of interesting tidbits, and one overwhelming observation: *they're clueless.* A survey, issued by Epsilon, a marketing services company, gives us a frightening glimpse into what CMOs are thinking, like:

- Apple is the only company in existence that knows how to "do marketing." It ranked higher than the muddle of second-tier companies by a factor of 6. This is intriguing, since Apple 1) doesn't buy in to, or practice any, precept of marketing as we know it, and b) it doesn't even have a CMO.

- The majority of survey respondents preferred John McCain for President. Interpret that as you wish.

- A third of the CMOs surveyed were "somewhat unsatisfied" with the job applicant pool these days, citing "creative thinking" as the most important quality the job-seekers lacked (70%). This observation comes in spite of the literal mad horde of unemployed marketers trolling the online classifieds for jobs they're overqualified to perform. And with technology, distribution, science, and loads of other pursuits encroaching on marketing's domain, the most important quality in a new hire is creativity?

- 86% of CMOs are satisfied, at least somewhat, with their primary external agencies. No, I'm not kidding. I suspect it has something to do with tickets to sporting events, as it can't have any relationship to business results.

This is some truly scary stuff, but if you ever read the pages of *Brandweek*, you're used to it by now. I have to remind myself that these are the types of people who are busy giving us Super Bowl ads and branded social media. They play their latest creative conceits and quack science playthings for one another as if it weren't utterly irrelevant, then talk about "return on investment" and "innovation" as consumers continue to tune out, shut down, and stop buying.

In other words, they're madly keeping the trains running on time as the Allied armies approach; or, more kindly, they want to make sure that the post-iceberg seating arrangements on the Titanic are done properly. The war is over, the ship is sinking, and they should be feverishly challenging and redefining everything...the "what" of a good vs. bad job applicant, the idea that any agency is doing a satisfactory job...in fact, they should be discovering what is "satisfactory" in a marketplace that values branding at $0?

This survey is just further evidence that they're clueless.

(64) Intention or Sneeze?

For those of you mapping your next branding campaign based on the insights of fMRI imaging, you better make sure that the flashes you're seeing aren't the symptoms of hay fever. Only you can't.

Functional Magnetic Resonance Imaging (fMRI) has been a *topic du jour* in the marketing world, as it promises to let us use brain scans to prove the efficacy of one branding message over another. Finally, there's scientific proof of all the mental images and emotions that we'd only been able to see indirectly via qualitative research. fMRI means you don't have to ask people what they think. You can just check the monitor, and adjust your marketing accordingly.

Only you can't.

The primary tool for this imaging is something called BOLD, for Blood-Oxygen-Level Dependent, as it allows for the measurement of the oxygen that neurons need when they fire. So it's an indirect measure, and it can get prompted by physiological prompts, including sinus pressure. It's also dependent on other chemicals present in a brain, it changes with familiarity, and it's based on measuring triggers for oxygen when the brain is prompted...and not when it prompts thoughts (or actions). On the macro-level at which we marketers live, this means we can see when and where brains flash when we run a commercial, or make a specific sales pitch, but there's no way to differentiate the substance of those flashes from, say, the enabling effects of a neurotransmitter, or the fact that somebody felt like they were about sneeze. It's all the same flash, irrespective of input or any future state.

Lots of correlative assumptions can get made about what the flashes might mean, but it's interpretation. Flashes indirectly prove that a brain responded to *stimuli*. Full stop. There's no suggestion (beyond more interpretation and hope) that said flashes connect in any way to subsequent thoughts (which can't be measured) or actions. Coke commercials don't flash red, or Pepsi blue. It would be really cool if you could make those links.

Only you can't.

The scientific community is so not in agreement about how to interpret fMRI to make its immediate applications to marketing little more reliable than using séances or phrenology.

So why do marketers even indulge in conversations about it, especially since there are such rich, obvious, and absolutely real tools of behavior available to decipher, map, and manage outbound marketing? Well, first, because it's totally cool. Understanding the biological basis for consciousness and sense of self, let alone branding, is really, really interesting. There's serious stuff to be learned about bridging the gap Descartes saw between mind and body. I'm all for it.

Second, marketers are poets, not scientists, and we believe our purpose is to influence perceptions and intent. Mind states matter more than actions, so we leave that behavioral stuff to sales people or, at best, our lesser cousins in direct marketing. fMRI plays to our predisposed interests. It proves our predispositions.

But I suspect the reason we're entertaining the nonsense about reading minds is because of the crisis in our industry.

Consumers are harder to reach, more difficult to convince, and nearly impossible to keep loyal. Every conceivable pressure is being applied to marketers...forcing proof that our marketing and branding efforts have any connection to the survival of our companies and clients.

So fMRI looks, feels, and purports to provide that proof – in a cool way, and of mental stuff that's far more important than physical reality – so you can claim that you're truly connecting with a consumer.

Only you can't. Flashes are as much proof that someone needs your brand as they reveal her need for a decongestant.

(65) See What You Wanna See

About halfway through the sophistic 1970's cartoon *The Point*, Oblio (the protagonist) encounters a man made out rock, and asks him in so many words the meaning of life.

"You see what you wanna see," says the Rock Man, "and hear what you wanna hear." The point of life is to stop looking for The Point, or to fit in, and pretty much decide what is important to you and, *voila!* You discovered the point after all.

This pot-addled treatise presaged the wilderness of social media in which so many companies are wandering these days. Only there are many, many rock men ready to dispense pop wisdom: Vitrue is one of the many agencies happy to take corporate marketing dollars to propagate social goodness into cyberspace. What caught my eye recently was its "Vitrue 100," which ranks brand names by how frequently they appear in blogs, chat rooms, forums, multimedia-sharing sites, etc. A higher position is good, as the tracking "... represents companies who are establishing their social presence and doing so successfully."

There's no qualification based on topic, issue, relevance, or purpose, or any other quality of conversation other than, well, *conversation.* The rankings aren't correlated with the mundane quantities that add up to real-world existence, like products getting shipped or returned...or money actually changing hands.

You see what you wanna see.

It seems that the most compelling reason many companies even consider doing social media campaigns is because 1) other companies have done so (it's cheaper than creating and running a TV commercial, for instance), and/or b) you don't really have to sell anything, so it's easier to do, too. "Being social" has its own set of rules and rewards. Books and workshops galore will gladly walk the willing through the steps necessary to conduct social campaigns correctly.

Sounds like the nonsense we were told during the CRM boom a few years ago. Everybody needed the software, and then pretty much nobody installed or used it correctly, or so the salesmen and gurus told us.

Like CRM, social media are newfangled enablers of activities that are about as old as Sanskrit. So the idea that they require the rejection of proven, truisms of human nature and behavior – or at least that everyone involved learn to ignore them – is kind of laughable. Businesses need to sell, and consumers need reasons to buy. Anything that doesn't somehow address these needs, no matter how entertaining or "engaging" risks being a distraction, at best, or a detraction, at worst.

That's the ultimate point, and it's been that way for a long, long time. A listing of product or company name mentions in social media is rather pointless, isn't it?

(66) In Praise of Lag

The Greek Chorus of technologists and the digerati continue to belittle marketers for their slowness in shifting ad budgets online.

The rationale is that 2/3 of consumers now use social networks for something or another, and online and portable music usage has soared. et 4 out of every 5 ad executives polled in a survey conducted by IBM said that they were "...at least five years away from being able to deliver cross-platform advertising, encompassing sales, delivery, measurement and analysis."

"Marketers don't have to wait five more years only to realize that they are now twenty years behind," explains one expert, with some disdain. "Everyone – both on the agency and client side – can fix this laggard attitude starting right now."

If anyone else claimed that the solution to a problem was 1) do something entirely logically flawed and untested, and 2) spend lots of money on it right away, they'd be laughed out of the room. When it comes to marketing ideas, however, we still give such nonsense credence, as if the insistent conclusions of their promoters are objective or true.

They're not. So I say congratulations to any marketer who has the fortitude to resist the siren call of cross-platform advertising, encompassing sales, delivery, measurement and analysis.

The strategy and content of brands emerged in lock-step with the technology available to reach consumers: distribution of news/entertainment via mass media print, followed by radio and television, allowed marketers of the 20th Century to present vague, emotionally-based promises before an audience of consumers who'd been trained to believe and follow. Image was reality, and the pretense flourished for at least a generation.

But those days are long gone. Reality begets image – first, foremost, and continuously – thanks to the Internet, and to our new-found "old" habit of relying on one another for info and affirmation. That means the ideas used to communicate with consumers can't just be adapted to digital tools, but need to be utterly redefined. The idea that brands (and their advertising) should be migrated online is like saying buggy whips should be reformatted for automobiles.

When Marshall McLuhan said "the medium is the message," he was partially correct: the way we interact with electronic media is as formative to our experience as the content delivered thereby. Ads may never work on Facebook because we're simply not there to read or care about them, just as faux billboards or other product placements in video games might prove unmemorable (just as they do in the real world, strangely enough).

Yet now know that *the message is the message, too.* Content matters. So when claims of new and improved fall on deaf ears in TV or print ads, it's not because of a failure of the medium, but rather the message; people haven't rejected advertising as much as tuned out the stuff that doesn't tell them anything relevant.

Similarly, when it comes to social media, it means that we have far to go in understanding the utility and practice of behavioral outcomes. Social networks require social activities as their *lingua franca*, but said activities need some ultimate purpose beyond, well, being activities. Underlying the digerati idea of brands is that branding should consist of people talking about branding.

How gloriously circular, and ultimately pointless. Digital engagement without actionable outcomes (other than more engagement) is no better than analog navel-gazing.

It makes sense that marketers are leery of these pitches. I wouldn't blame their fear, or laziness, or lack of futuristic vision. Maybe they're aware, however viscerally, that there's an absence in all of the guru disdain of any substantive and meaningful conversation about what, when, how, why, and if doing it makes sense.

Online delivery of cross-platform advertising, encompassing sales, delivery, measurement and analysis isn't a foregone conclusion...it's a question in need of answers. Perhaps the best way to explore it isn't to "fix this laggard attitude." I'm all for some responsible, thoughtful lag.

(67) Transformation Interrupted

According to market research firm Hartman Group, consumer loyalty is shifting – from products and brands, to the experiences offered by retailers – in a radical transformation that started before the recession. I think the change is much bigger than that.

Hartman is onto something because it specializes in ethnographic market research (among other tools), which is an attempt to understand consumers in the context of their lives, both in terms of their knowledge and beliefs, and through their behaviors. I believe the firm is saying that capturing consumers' attention with creative and/or compelling marketing communications no longer carries the water in our busy, confused, noisy lives; experiences are what stick, bring differences into sharp focus, and compel purchases.

The problem is that retailers can't "own" experiences or, more broadly, experience is a synonym for the context of reality. The more people know, or think they know, the less they believe (broadly), and more tenaciously hold onto what little they do (specifically). This is the intriguing dichotomy of our Internet Age; as consumers gain the capacity to explore and share, they lose the ability to trust and commit. Institutions are no longer credible, and historic truths aren't reliable; facts and fiction are endlessly available, and often impossible to tell apart; every subject is up for discussion and debate, which occurs in real-time, all the time.

No wonder people aren't willing to buy based on the intangibles on which brands have relied for almost a Century. Reality is the new imagination, providing the context in which actions can assert truth (if not simply immediacy, and thus clarity) to consumers. This idea isn't limited to retailers; the challenge is for any business to make what it does, not just what it says, believable and compelling. Actions, and the myriad of experiences they enable – from in-store environments, online glimpses of manufacturing, policy decisions, to the behavior of every employee and vendor, whether at work or not – are what feed awareness, conversation, and thus brands.

Brands exist in this reality of experience. Communications can describe it, but marketing can no longer serve as a substitute or dictation for it. It's a great opportunity, and it's bigger than, say, a social media strategy, or something that's experiential and in-store. These are tactics. The radical transformation underway in the marketplace started before the meltdown, and it's inevitably changing the very substance of what marketers do for a living.

The recession was a brief interruption. The challenge is to see past it.

(68) What Do They Know?

More companies are declining to provide revenue or earnings estimates for their next three months of business. This is a disturbing trend that reveals a scary vacuum at the core of their strategic planning processes. Two bits of recent research illustrate the problem:

- A third of the 600 companies responding to a survey by the National Investor Relations Institute said they'd limited or eliminated their forward-looking guidance.

- Almost two-thirds of companies cannot accurately forecast cash flow within 10 percent, according to a study by a management consulting firm called The Hackett Group, Inc.

So Intel declined to give any guidance a week ago on its upcoming quarter. Manpower Inc. did, too. BMW and SAP put up their collective financial hands and gave up on predicting the end of 2008...in November! A host of retailers have not only retired from providing forward-looking predictions, but have stopped reporting past month sales results (such as Macy's, Home Depot, Sears, and CVS Caremark).

Why the cloudy corporate crystal balls? The current credit crunch, fickle customer demand, and other externalities that, according to the NIRI's CEO, means "If you don't know what the future holds and you can't accurately predict it, you don't want to be out there telling somebody something you don't have confidence in."

The laws of physics render the future an unknowable destination, so forecasts are the paths we follow to find it. Businesses rely on forecasts for every function, from ordering parts/ingredients for products and hiring/training staff, to borrowing cash and making investment decisions. They do it all the time, so a claim that even the immediate tomorrow is somehow beyond the purview of a strategic planning model must mean:

- The company doesn't like what it sees, which means investors should be frightened, and/or

- It really doesn't know how to deliver on its plans, which should send everyone running away, screaming.

If the news looks like it's going to be bad, shouldn't a company be required to share insights as to why things might look that way, and what actions it will take to impact it? The tools exist to collect and analyze more information in an instant than most individuals can absorb in a lifetime, and we're supposed to believe that the CEO has *no* visibility?

Now, if that visibility is really and truly cloudy, and the business can't specify the activities it can rely upon (i.e. the reliable core of its plans that it can all but guarantee), doesn't that say something about a vacuum at the very core of its strategy? Companies are responsible for understanding not just what should happen, but what they can make happen, while assigning meaning to it all. If the future is really a blank slate, the management should be fired, or the company simply boarded up. Jeez...even blackjack players assign percentage likelihoods to cards yet to appear face-up on the table.

It's simply unreasonable for brand names to reduce perceptions of the fundamental drivers of corporate performance – revenue and profits – to the equivalent of a shrug.

I know, I know, Wall Street stock analysts are mean and unforgiving, and they punish companies if they miss their estimates by even a small fraction. I say deal with it. Everybody knows that you can't guarantee what the future may hold. We already know what should work might not work out. Businesses are in business to hatch plans, and then deliver them, and they have a responsibility to communicate to us what is a core, reliable plan, and what variables may affect it.

That is...presuming they know.

(69) The Superbrands Discount

Brandweek has listed America's Top 2000 Brands. It's an approximate measure, for sure, coming from some organization called Superbrands, but so is the overall concept of brand itself. While most analyses of branding get all caught up in qualitative measures, at least this list is based on a quantitative fact that's elegantly simple:

The top brands are the brands that spend the most on branding.

Who said you couldn't buy your way to popularity? Brands as the business corollary of Paris Hilton's fame. I love it. No wonder we need exotic sensing devices and anti-Boolean variables to explain what all that spending buys.

A number of *other* measures might be more useful in determining whether spending on branding was worth it. Brand equity should be a real factor in influencing costs of other corporate activities; here are three for-instances:

1. CAGR (more brand equity should lower cost to get on shelf).

2. Average Salary (employees should trade some % of salary for benefit of working for a great brand name).

3. Product Development (richer brands should yield new products/extensions faster).

Oh, here's another measure: *sales*. And another: *profits*. Superbrands should be able to sell easier/better/more often, and do so at a high profit margin than lesser brands, right? If so, the really meaningful measures of brands wouldn't be aggregate expenditures, but rather strategic benefit or return, calculated in dollars, pounds, yen, or whatever.

But for now, we've got the Superbrands ranking, and I've been struggling to come up with a productive use for it. I think I've got it: discount companies that top this list. More brand spending means they probably don't have a clue about what really drives consumer preference and loyalty. Practice a little risk assessment here; more willingness to spend on the vagaries of brand might very well mean less ability (or willingness) to focus on more important drivers of performance.

Call it *The Superbrands Discount*...perhaps gin up a thumbnail equation, like profits/branding expenditure...and assign a % discount to the stock price accordingly. A higher profit-to-brand ratio is not a good thing?

(70) Twitter, The Poetry of Love

Nielsen Online released a report in late April, in which it argued that usage rates for new Twitter users dropped precipitously after the first month, and that this meant its growth didn't match the early adoption rates of Facebook or MySpace.

Reaction to the study predictably fell into two groups: those who'd given up on Twitter (or avoided it altogether because of its reputation), and those who were offended that anybody would even suggest that it wasn't something truly great. The critics seemed cool and smug; its defenders were passionately insulted.

So I've got it: Twitter isn't a technology, or a service, so tracking the numbers could never really add up correctly. After reading all of the commentary, I understand that numbers will never capture the meaning of the phenomenon, because Twitter is more like *love*. You either feel it, or you don't. Here are six reasons why Twitter and love are similar

- They're best described by analogies that far surpass the inadequacy of the literal descriptions. Literally, Twitter is "a 140 character message distribution platform," and love is "the positive feelings two people have for one another." But the descriptions that mean more to folks are Twitter's ambient awareness, and love's eternal bonds.

- Those amorphous descriptions are also utterly unknowable. I use Twitter for reasons that are mine alone, just as my experience of love is very personal. We might think we share an understanding of what we're talking about, but we really only share the desire to share it. And we share our knowledge that we "get it," as you have to tweet to understand Twitter, just like you have to love to truly fathom it.

- Our feelings are mutually-exclusive; technically, you can't use Twitter like I do, because you're not me. Ditto for my expressing love the same way that you do.

- Our experiences are self-referencing. The most productive conversations via social media are conversations about social media. Similarly, love is best described as a thing, almost a state of being.

- Both Twitter and love are about breaking rules. Twitter works because something doesn't work (like customer service), so it strikes out on its own, making up new rules as it goes along. Sounds like the technical corollary of "...wrap[ping] your legs around these velvet rims, and strap[ping] your hands across my engines," doesn't it? Both let users skip out on humdrum, everyday life.

- Love and Twitter aren't easy. You have to try and fail at both to really comprehend what they mean. Both involve breakups...Twitter with followers who are stalkers, and followees who just aren't interesting, and love with, well, you know the deal, most probably.

So I say we stop all this nonsense about metrics and the other frail, limited attempts to constrain our experience of Twitter. A fad by any other name would smell as tweet?

Just For Fun: Entanglement

Researchers have recently proven that a quality of the unseen quantum world called "entanglement" can happen also at the microscopic level (i.e. the size of stuff in the regular world).

Entanglement is really strange: what happens is that two particles can get mated (how that happens is a bit of a mystery), and then communicate with one another not just faster than the speed of light, but instantaneously. This is a really, really big mystery, because it violates a few cardinal laws of physics: nothing can travel faster than the speed of light, at which point an object's mass should become infinite. And since light itself has a speed, being instantaneous is something that just doesn't happen in Einstein's relative universe.

There's some explanation of why such strangeness is possible, as per the hints contained in the enabling math. But there's absolutely no answer for *how*.

It helps that most activity at the quantum level is really weird. It turns out that everything there doesn't really exist at all, *per se*, but rather hovers in a state on indeterminacy, only collapsing into something observable when somebody observes it. Observation is a core quality of what reality is made of, according to quantum physics. Let's not even get started on the multiple dimensions...

Now, scientists have reported in *Nature* that they've entangled pairs of beryllium and magnesium ions, and they've exhibited the same qualities of entanglement. This means that the real world is as strange as the quantum one.

I'd say we've seen it already in politics and business for a while already. The Democrats and Republicans are entangled, aren't they? One of the qualities of entanglement is that objects are the opposite of one another (one particle spins left, so the other always spins right). Coke and Pepsi were entangled for many years, so just as one brand would announce some starlet, the other had a competing celeb ready to announce, too. And, just for kicks, isn't our experience of Internet Search the macro version of that observation thing I mentioned earlier? We invent reality from the cloud with our choice of search terms...

Maybe the bigger observation from this entanglement research is that there are really strange forces going on, and that seeing them – and even describing them with some detail and reliability – doesn't mean that we understand what's going on.

Chapter Eight
What Were They Thinking?

It's hard not to dish on some of the year's deliciously insane marketing ideas.

The funny thing is that many of them could have been really smart. Whether small and just silly, or enormously stupid, much of went on in 2009 was more like tragedy than comedy.

What was the difference between the home runs and the numbnut ideas? *Misplaced vision* was the single most common point. Marketers set out to accomplish things, often establishing very clear purposes and expectations for their activities. Then they executed against those plans...only a lot of the goals were just wrong.

The worst examples were those that did the absolute best jobs of accomplishing the wrong things. They were also probably some of the examples that were heralded in the mainstream business media as great successes.

I'm not sure the media have caught up with what's going on; many businesses surely haven't. There's a shift that's been going on since before the recent economic woes, and I've long believed that marketers have been slow to acknowledge and respond to an emergent fact that the changing technology and cultural landscape doesn't mean we need to do branding differently, but also that we need to come up with a different definition of brands altogether.

There are many brilliant, creative marketers still working to deliver on outdated expectations that brands are things people care about, depend upon, or otherwise maintain as deep psychological states. This old definition means that marketing's purpose is to *get people to think things*, and makes the time they spend doing so – irrespective of what exactly they're thinking about – an absolute benefit of branding.

A solid chain of strategic vision stretches from Texaco sponsoring Milton Berle's radio show in the 1930s, to Burger King paying for a "friending" promotion on Facebook in 2009. Different media, and different content. Same intention. Same definition of brands.

But not the same reaction from consumers, who keep getting harder to find and talk with, more suspicious of what they're being told, less likely to buy what and when we want them to (and at the prices we wish), and almost never loyal.

I'm all for a snippy laugh about bad marketing, but it's a bit biting when so much of it was simply really good at pursuing a bad idea. Hence the tragedy. So here's what I think these examples from 2009 tell us about how to look at brands, and how we go about translating that POV into effective marketing communications in 2010 and beyond:

1. **Doing beats thinking.** A fundamental disconnect between old and new definitions of brand center on measurement; whether it's worthwhile to hope people think something, or whether it makes more sense to focus on prompting behaviors. Just like many of the year's home runs did the latter, I think the dumbest ones were those that successfully got people to think something (for a moment, if little else).

2. **Need is more important than want.** No matter how entertaining some of the year's spots (or campaigns) might have been, they were ultimately losers if they didn't address a consumer *need* instead of simply trying to promote a desire, or *want*. My guess is that purchase behavior isn't going back to the profligate ways of the past decade; if people don't need something, they very well might not buy it.

3. **Marketing doesn't own marketing.** When you look at your dedicated marketing budget for 2010, consider all the money *other* corporate departments are spending, too...because a lot of what they do influences consumer perceptions and proclivities. Some of it is lots *more* important than what marketing says (corporate behavior matters more in social media than your ad creative). There's still no good model for mapping these dependencies, by the way.

4. **Don't underestimate the impact of little things.** Big campaigns with big ideas talk about bigness, yet it is often the little thing – a contextual conflict, or fact that didn't substantiate the big claims – that makes them inert.

5. Selling irrelevant stuff is irrelevant. If we added up the marketing budgets for the top ten most expensive branding campaigns in 2009, you'd have to conclude that the most important themes to communicate were various complicated corollaries of a fart joke.

6. So never trade "funny" for some imaginary engagement. Talk about your business. My agency friends will sometimes argue otherwise, but I don't think any recent marketing activity substantiated the proposition that you can associate your product or service with some external emotion or experience (like being funny) or that it does anything permanent (or motivating to subsequent sales). If you're going to spend money, why not spend it to talk about your business?

7. Be obvious. Consumers on average spend something like a nano-second paying attention to whatever it is you're throwing at them, even if your reports say that they spent a half hour watching your brilliant viral video. They weren't conscious for most of it. 2010 will require us to make sure we use the little time we have to talk with more judicious thinking (more relevance, meaning, and immediate utility). Think of a fart joke if you must, but add a payoff of action other than a good laugh.

8. Acknowledge context. I think some really dumb activities were really smart, but only if you experienced them in a vacuum separate from any real time or place. There's a "looked so good in the conference room presentation" phenomenon that dooms so much stuff, especially when the creative requires that people 'get' things like interaction and/or jokes. See point 7.

9. Don't drink your own Kool-Aid. I don't know how we could ever measure brands by asking consumers explicit questions about what they think about branding. It's marvelously circular logic, isn't it? See point 10.

10. Sales are what matter. You already know this if you've cut a marketing budget (or had yours slashed). Selling is the ultimate purpose of having a brand, doing branding, or spending anything on marketing, so you're not going to have the time in 2010 (let alone the reasonable hope) to wait for awareness or some other squishy measure of communications efficacy to pay off.

Here are essays on some of the most deliciously terrible marketing events for you to consider avoiding:

(71) Lost In Branding-Land

Now that GM is out of bankruptcy, it's still spending approximately $50 million per month to run its "Reinvention" spots. If the recent emergence took 9 months to accomplish, the branding campaign presumes to close the door on 100 years of history in 30 seconds.

Actually, the pivot comes less than 15 seconds into the piece, when the narrator has noted mistakes, errors, or some other coded references to having sucked up $50 billion-plus in taxpayer money (and then going bankrupt because of its employee-related costs). Then, it's enough with history; the company is focused on the future, and is already fast at work creating a newer, smarter, less apology-prone business.

Added to the latest nonsense about a "green" logo (a conversation that doesn't happen without lots of pricey expert help), it's obvious that GM is a company lost in branding-land.

I can imagine the meetings at which it was decided that an apology was somehow necessary. 'm sure the qualitative research told them that we let consumers down was a sentiment that should resonate with people who've not bought a GM car lately; it's not that they chose other makes, but rather that the company failed to win them over, and for that, it needs to be sorry. Once it acknowledges this reality, its subsequent claims will be far more relevant and credible.

Only it isn't reality.

GM failed its employees, suppliers, dealers, and investors. It mismanaged their hard work, mishandled their relationships, mistakenly abused their initiative, and mistook their inertia for confidence. Any apology should have been directed at these audiences first, if not solely.

But for them, an apology wouldn't be enough, nor would the claims of the next phase of GM's branding campaign, which purportedly will start running now that it's out of bankruptcy; it's going to declare a "new" GM, and you can bet that it'll be chocked full of that faux populist rhetoric that only a truly inspired copywriter could scribble. New focus. New spirit. New *new*, with some more new added for newness.

It took 100 years to drive this great company into the ground, and we're supposed to believe that it only took 9 months to create an entirely new entity? That's not real, it's surreal. Worse, it smacks of being a lie.

The branding campaign is evidence that it's business as usual at GM, at least in the marketing department. No matter how it gets presented – whether via glossy videos on TV, or lots of viral video and the other detritus of social media – it tells us that the company either doesn't know, or doesn't care what it needs to do before it can claim to tell us anything believable:

- Tell us with specific examples how there's a new partnership with employees, after hammering the unions for zillions of givebacks.

- Explain what has been done on the assembly-line floors to ensure that they build will be de facto superior to any other.

- Describe the truly innovative ways that the dealer network has been strengthened, not just thinned.

- Provide tangible examples of the supplier commitment from companies large and small across America.

- Give investors a new understanding of what it means to own GM stock, and how the company will ensure more transparency and knowledge.

If GM is doing these things right now, you wouldn't know it, would you? If it is, it could use these real actions as the basis for its repositioning to consumers.

A truly "new" GM would skip the slickly-produced apology ads, and avoid declaring anything (Chrysler did the "new" thing a few months before admitting it couldn't make a car worth selling any longer)...and instead address the reality of why car buyers should join it in the adventure. Invite them to participate in the reinvention. Narrate the process, honestly an explicitly. Don't produce an inspiring branding campaign; rather, invent a truly new approach to the what and then how of stakeholder engagement.

There's no "new" GM without a fundamentally new approach to its marketing. A social media campaign doesn't count, and great ad creative won't cut it. It's just more of the same old nonsense.

(72) Hope For Twinkies?

Interstate Bakeries, the maker of such Boomer staples as Twinkies and Wonder Bread, is emerging from a four-year stint in bankruptcy, with a plan to compete, innovate, and implement new methods of distribution.

If there's any hope for the business, I sure hope they leave their brand experts in the courtroom. Preferably under lock and key.

Interstate is responsible for giving a generation of consumers two major benefits:

1. Soggy, milk-white sandwich bread that let shine the filling (which was usually some pressed-beef product or, if you were lucky, Fluff).
2. A high-calorie, trans-fat rich delivery vehicle cleverly disguised as a snack product.

The stuff tasted so good because it was bad for you, triggering all of those receptors in our minds and stomachs that starving for eons of evolution had put there to tell us when we'd tripped over sources of dense nourishment. Unfortunately, since we're no longer terrorized primates who run for our lives for a living, it was inevitable that we'd realize that bad stuff wasn't too good for us.

So then the inevitable branding answers followed: "lite" versions of Twinkie snacks, portion and packaging changes, even "whole wheat Wonder Bread." If consumers wanted healthy, Interstate would comply.

Yuck. In doing so, it gave up the very reasons anybody would want to buy the stuff. *Bad is good*, as anybody will admit, either publicly, or to one's inner sneak. At least sometimes. A healthy Wonder Bread or Twinkies product makes about as much sense as candy-coated broccoli. Cognitive dissonance would be an improvement.

What should Interstate do to stay in business? I'm hopeful that there's a lot of thinking behind its brief public statements (and beyond the prerequisite plans to clobber union workers):

• Innovation. I say stop destroying the fundamental benefits of Wonder Bread, Hostess, and its other brands, and innovate against the goal of making it easier, faster, more affordable, and more likely that people will buy the stuff *because it's bad for them*. Healthy alternative? Nobody needs it. We need joy and guilty pleasures in our lives.

• Reinvigorate its brands. The nostalgia angle to sell to Boomers is getting a bit old, and it's starting to grate (we could live without Dennis Hopper selling financial services, or some tone-deaf singer destroying a Bowie song to help fail to sell Lincolns). Twinkie doesn't need to remind anyone over the age of 30 what it is; the brand failed to ever escape its reputation. So be real, and be current.

- Find new distribution. So much of what we attribute to brand preference is really the habit or routines of consumption. Are there better ways to get snacks to people other than stacking them on grocery shelves? Of course. Interstate needs to think less about telling the world about its brand attributes, and creating more consumption moments.

None of these changes needed to wait for the blessing of a bankruptcy judge; other than freeing up funds (not a small accomplishment, I know), the keepers of the brands could have been pushing the actions for years. Only they didn't, opting instead for lots of traditional brand marketing nonsense, which succeeded only in dismantling its once-relevant products...all in the name of staying relevant!

There might be hope yet for Twinkies if they leave those marketers – and their outdated ideas about brands – in the past. Now, if only somebody would make Space Food Sticks mainstream again.

(73) Unstuck from the Middle

For all of the news about Google's implicit threat to evict ad agencies from their traditional role as go-betweens for clients and their commercial content, now publishers of all types are getting in on the game.

The Conde Nast New Media Group has produced a print spread for LG Electronics featuring director Edward Zwick. It's utterly forgettable in the same way the other famous people slice-of-life vignettes always are, like those from American Express. It's visually about a guy who looks bored, or was dumb enough to bring along his TV set-up on a camping trip. The header – "Life is Good" – is generic to the point of being an insult, and I think a T-shirt company already uses the line.

What's notable isn't that a publisher could produce utter garbage just like an ad agency would if given the chance, but rather that it seized the chance in the first place.

If they can't act as the middleman between clients and ads, whether digital or otherwise, what's left for the ad agencies to do? WPP's Mindshare bought the space, and publicly blathered on with the usual nonsense about Conde being "a premium brand." It seems to have also successfully convinced its client to believe that such inert content makes a "human, emotional connection to the brand." But, ultimately, the campaign relegates the agency to the role of real estate broker, hoping to sell a house that has already been built and decorated. I can already hear David Ogilvy rolling over in his grave.

Play out the agency trend to its logical conclusion, and you get something like this:

- The middlemen get squeezed out of the steps separating clients and the delivery of marketing content.

- All costs are reduced thereby, so there exists a truly efficient system to conceive and place ads (this is the Google model, as the ad content will be based on presumed behavioral clicking predictions gleaned from past clicks).

- Once the transformation is complete, we discover a deeper, more fundamental problem: people don't relate to brands in the psychobabble, ephemeral ways that we once thought (or hoped) that they did.

- Ads that don't do anything to directly impact sales, whether immediately or casually somehow, are still ineffective, no matter how efficiently they're delivered.

The LG experiment is not an example of a shining, new future for advertising, but rather proof that agencies could be well on the way to becoming unnecessary middlemen. Google and its brethren stealing money to buy search terms and clicks. Publishers creating ads directly for clients. It doesn't bode well for the long term, just as the stupid ad itself will do absolutely nothing for LG in the short-term.

(74) Ask is Still Searching

Ask's latest branding campaign is intended to frighten or offend most of its potential customers. It does the job brilliantly.

The TV spots feature some nerdy guy with his chin resting on a pregnant woman's shoulder, whether she's walking down the street or lying in bed. He asks questions that she might predictably ask. The punchline is that Ask.com will help you find the answers.

To say that it's creepy is an understatement, especially when the guy in bed is wondering aloud if it's ok for the would-be mom to have sex with her partner. It's also insulting, as he's obviously ethnic (for some incomprehensible reason), which makes Motrin's baby sling campaign (which drove this week's Twitterfest of hate) seem like a downright compliment to all of womanhood.

I can't imagine why the braintrust at Ask would think that there's a brand attribute in Internet search more important than accuracy or utility. Maybe that's what they're trying to get at with the campaign, but the message is obfuscated by all the creative and complex nonsense that brand experts regularly wrap around otherwise simple ideas.

Ask can't make the case for why its search is better, faster, easier, or otherwise different from Google, Yahoo, MSN, or any number of lesser entrants in the category; it must instead make a statement about its brand.

Talk about a search query that turns up snake eyes.

Watching TV is kind of like aimless search, in that the consumer is somewhat aware and/or receptive to getting information, even if he or she wasn't necessarily actively looking for it. That's the premise behind advertising overall: throw stuff at people who broadly might possess some willingness to buy your stuff, and hope that whatever it is you're telling them catches them at the right moment to actually register.

And an ad...any ad...has a really limited amount of time in which to earn that attention, as well as implant an idea that'll get used later on. Or prompt an action that'll be more immediate (call, write, inquire, whatever). In this sense, all advertising is direct, ultimately, even if all it asks you to do is to remember the content.

Ask's challenge to use this nanosecond it captures of your our attention to communicate that it provides better search. There are probably lots of ways to make this care, many of them really fun and creative. But the overarching goal is to make that case in a simple, unambiguous way. There's little reason to do much else.

So what's Ask's branding answer? It wants you to remember the creepy guy. Or get offended because he's a stereotype of one sort or another. In this way, the brand fails to deliver on the very premise of its campaign. It can't even ask the right question it should endeavor to answer: how do we attract new users?

(75) Go Steal Some Customers

Last Friday, Sprint announced that it had lost another 1.3 million subscribers, and turned in a quarterly loss of $326 million. It promised to boost ad spending. Company CEO Dan Hesse said they'd "make the case for competitive pricing." He's been the spokesperson in some of the ads so far.

Maybe I'm missing something, but who cares about a generic white guy declaring to the world that his phone costs the same as everyone else's?

Sprint needs to go steal some customers from the companies that have been poaching them. AT&T. Verizon. T-Mobile. Instead, we get word of a new branding angle – they're shifting their positioning from "lifestyle" to "value," whatever that means – as if anybody cares. Value in the mobile phone business means the lowest possible prices, usually combined with the greatest amount of obfuscation and complexity in usage reporting. Cool phones and ephemeral price promos prompt switching, and then customers get busy hating their service.

Branding? The mobile phone business is about as close as you can get to a knife fight in the street without 1) fighting with a knife, and 2) being in the street.

Worse, the weekend of its business announcement, Sprint sponsored the *Half Time Reports* on Fox TV's football shows. What that has to do with stealing customers, I have no idea. Maybe it makes sense for the brand positioning on some PowerPoint slide. And remember, these are the branding experts who gave us those flashlight commercials with people drawing cool shapes in the air. Relevance to switching phone carriers? Not so much. Great for flashlight makers, though.

Instead of talking about positioning and faux catchy slogans (theirs is "Simply Everything"), wouldn't it make much more sense for Sprint to target the behavioral triggers that'll get them some customers? Here are a few ideas Sprint might want to spend money on...and skip some of the branding nonsense:

- Give some group of "winners" a year of unlimited phone use. Blunt, brass-tacks promotional marketing would let contestants (or sign-ups in, say, December) qualify to win a 2009 of free use. For that matter, why not do it every year, and one of the benefits of being a Sprint member is qualifying for that drawing on an annual basis?

- Offer a better bounty for switchers. More in-your-face marketing might inspire people not only to switch, but incentivize them to bring their friends. Maybe groups of people qualify for bulk discounts (a friends-and-family mini-network pricing structure?), or at least Sprint could make its word-of-mouth aspirations more financially lucrative to the would-be talkers.

- Declare usage goals and track progress. Maybe Sprint needs to quantify what "success" means, and thus make success its primary brand attribute? So name the # of customers its wants, announce its progress every month (or week, or whatever), and invent incentives/rewards for the entire user community as they progress along the path (or add them if progress falters).

Dire circumstances require true invention, not just mouthing the right words about brand and spending. Wasting more money on marketing that hasn't worked so far is a pretty dim bulb thing to do. Branding emerges from the business, not versa visa, so why not create a marketing strategy that is driven by actual company behaviors, and that offers actual, real benefits to phone users? Sprint needs to stop branding and go steal some customers.

(76) Your Name Here

In the novel *Infinite Jest*, author David Foster Wallace invented a hilarious, if not somewhat frightening future, in which corporations could sponsor pretty much every aspect of life, up to underwriting years of the calendar. Much of the book takes place during the *Year of the Depend Undergarment*.

I'm thinking maybe he was more creative than prescient (and, sadly, he's also dead, a victim by his own hand last year). The amounts of money spent on corporate sponsorships and celebrity endorsements would shock you if somebody handed you a list. Citi committed $400 million to put its name on the new Mets ballpark. AIG spends almost $100 million annually to have its logo on the jerseys of the Manchester United soccer team. GM paid Tiger Woods almost $60 million over the past decade to stand next to a Buick.

And for what? *Branding*, of course. The logic, if you can call it that, relies on the premise that you can:

- Associate disparate ideas, often by simply placing images or words next to one another.

- Deliver this information to consumers, usually by putting it in front of them, or hoping they'll see it as they drive by.

- Rely on consumers retaining this information, which can only be sensed via queries about that very information, via polls, focus groups, etc.

- Presume that they'll keep said information sacrosanct, and not modify or lose it based on other associations presented to them (incessantly so, by the way).

- Expect them to apply those remembered associations to their subsequent purchase decisions, whenever and wherever they might occur.

Can you imagine trying to draw that flowchart on a wall, let alone make the case for it, in front of a management team or board of directors living today?

I'd put sponsorships in the realm of *out there marketing*. No, not in the sense of being cutting-edge or strange, but rather because it requires that there's a *there* out there – somewhere – wherein these associations are forged, perpetuated, and used.

I expect that our current economic predicament is going to make the out there marketing approach a lot less attractive. The next year will most certainly have a sponsor, but it won't be Depends, or any other commercial enterprise. It'll be brought to us by something called *Necessity*. I think it might be called the *Year of Doing Things For Measurable Reasons*.

(77) Crashing Into Reality

Have you been following the branding imagery coming from Louis Vuitton lately?

There's a pretty severe "aspirational traveler" thing going on, first with print ads featuring folks like Keith Richards, Sean Connery, and Mikhail Gorbachev on the road, seated next to their Vuitton bags, and now a shot of former astronauts staring into space (and lots of videos extending the images into purposeless movies on the company web site).

The word "journey" keeps popping up in the copy, in various permutations, and the association is clear: add Vuitton luggage to your fantasies of travel to exotic places, whereby you'll do joyful or broadly important, global traveler sort of things. The Annie Leibovitz photos are full of, well, themselves, as usual.

I wonder how that's working for Vuitton?

The entire concept seems oddly detached from reality; not that the campaign needs to portray the ugly, messy, crowded reality for the vast majority of travelers who can't fly by private jet, but it still needs to exist in a reality in which awareness of that reality is a reality.

In other words, *travel sucks*. Buying the fantasy of Vuitton seems diametrically opposed to that fact, rendering it less a dream, and more a lie.

I would have imagined the campaign less about celebrities and these austere moments of reflection on the road (Sean Connery in a tree, Keith Richards in his luxury hotel room), and reflected instead some esoteric quality that Vuitton brings to the real travel experience. You know, that carrying the logo'd bag somehow insulates you from the unpleasantness of getting someplace; Vuitton is the tool – and therefore the badge – for people who rise above the circumstances, and achieve some higher, more profoundly cool state of being:

- You get through an airport security body cavity search with panache.
- Your bag stands out among all the soiled, bruised bags on the carousel.
- Taxis can fit your bag more easily; you're less likely to forget it
- Riff further, accordingly.

Don't give us these artsy-contrived stolen moments of famous people doing the cash-collecting things that famous people do...how about showing us folks, famous or not, navigating the trials and tribulations of existence... Vuitton being the key to transcending the here-and-now and achieving something truly...luxurious?

I just think that when this luxury positioning nonsense crashes into reality, reality wins.

(78) A Suicide Note

With once-great newspapers becoming extinct or, worse, going online in markets across the U.S., we've been given an interesting twist from a long-suffering paper in London: in *The Evening Standard* has spent the last month telling its readers that it's sorry.

I assume this will be followed by an announcement that it as emptied its last ink well, or broken the final printing press, or whatever. The branding campaign all but amounts to a very public suicide note.

Don't get me wrong, as I'm all for a well-meaning apology. Admitting guilt, even if it was more perceived than deserved, is a key way to resolve a conflict. An apology can right a wrong, or simply grease the mechanism of civility that's under fire in waiting lines, crowded street intersections, and the give-and-take of interpersonal relationships. Residents of Tokyo do it incessantly, as it helps them live closes together without killing one another.

So why is *The Evening Standard* apologizing to Londoners? Because it has been negative. Lost touch. Been predictable and complacent. You see, in holding focus groups, its ad agency discovered that younger readers perceive the brand as "right-wing," and feel that it is preoccupied with crime. The first leg of the branding campaign was to admit these faults in stark, explicit terms (see image above), and was followed by a second leg that made promises to "listen" and to "surprise." Part of the surprise will be the appearance of articles by expensive writers, like Tom Wolfe and Tom Stoppard.

What absolute rubbish, as they .say.

The problem for *The Evening Standard* is no different, broadly speaking, than the issues facing the *Boston Globe*, *New York Times*, or papers that have already evaporated into the ether (like the *Rocky Mountain News*): people don't feel compelled to read them. No amount of fond feelings or other perceptions will change that. In fact, I think most people like the idea of newspapers, kind of like they like the ideas of public television and diets. Good things, but honestly, they're not for me.

The London paper's vague apology and promise reveal that it hasn't figured out the problem. Readers don't need reasons to tolerate, like, or even adore *the Standard*. They need reasons to need the newspaper:

- What would it take to claim, truly, to be the "paper of record" for Londoners?

- How could it consistently deliver meaningful, exclusive perspective on the news?

- Where might it find affirmation of "truth," so its reporting was trusted above all others?

The Evening Standard needs to rethink its offering, and establish new criteria and tools for being indispensably relevant to its reader's lives. That's not a branding problem, *it's a business challenge*, and no marketing strategy can fix it. Newspapers all over the world are broken, but not lost beyond repair, and this paper is no exception.

Unless, of course, it thinks the answer is to try to be another entertainment medium. Then I'd say the ad campaign just served as its suicide note.

(79) Naming Rights Gone Wrong

"People are mistaken when they see tall buildings as symbols of a corporation," said a spokeswoman for Willis Group Holdings, which changed the name of Chicago's Sears Tower earlier this month. She's right. Willis made a big mistake.

Willis is a financial services company based in the UK. It's leasing 140,000 sq. ft. of space in the building, and naming rights came along with the deal. So it deleted the label that had been on the structure since its construction in 1973.

The Sears Tower is a landmark, branded by its very existence. A generation or two have grown up knowing it as such, even if we know that Sears doesn't have anything to do with it anymore (the company moved to smaller digs in the suburbs years ago). Maps, brochures, and countless family photo albums preserve the legacy.

I'm not sure what Willis accomplishes if it rewrites that recognition, presuming that it's even possible. I am sure that there's lots of blather from branding experts to conceptually support the hope. Perhaps Willis hopes to sell stuff directly to consumers. Maybe it needs to market itself to B2B partners and clients. Of all the ways available to tell the world what might be most important or relevant toward realizing these goals, the company chose to put its name on a skyscraper...and thus accomplished the same thing as doing so on a sports stadium: it declares authentic, credible, and that "we've arrived."

Or not. I'd suggest that it's more like the real estate corollary of a celebrity endorsement. The hope is that the brand can trade on the value (or awareness) of the physical property and, in this case, Willis hopes that it'll get recognition for, well, putting its name over the original name of a really tall building that everyone knows is named Sears. Maybe it'll pay off in 30 years, or however long it takes for everyone who remembers the Sears name to die.

The worst part of all this is that Willis missed an opportunity to really make a difference for its brand.

It turns out that it plans to pour zillions into making the building some green miracle, including installing a luxury hotel. It has already put in some gut-wrenching glass-bottomed observation deck. It's actually making the building very much different. The marketing strategy should have been to make all those changes and only then rename the structure. It would have been naming what had effectively become a new building, and been a platform to associating all those good, real-world improvements with the Willis name.

All the steps along the way would have generated interest and media coverage, thereby substantiating the ultimate anointing of the tower with a new label.

Unfortunately, it got its naming rights all wrong.

(80) This Mall Has...Stores!

Woodfield Mall, a shopping monolith to the west of Chicago, has launched a new branding campaign via its web site and print ads (I saw mine in the *Chicago Tribune's* Sunday magazine), to tell would-be shoppers something unique and motivational:

The mall has stores!

Yup. I know it's big, and the strategy probably took lots of work, and cost a lot, I'm sure. You don't just fall out of bed with this kind of idea, you know. The campaign is centered on six imaginary shoppers, each named and artistically rendered in funky drawings, who come with their own backstories, and lists of stores they like to visit.

These faux characters illustrate the mall's slogan – Everyone gets their own – and the idea of the branding is to hope you or I find our "match," and are thus inspired to visit the stores they like. I mean that their creators listed.

Doing the branding thing wasn't such a bad idea. It's just that this execution stinks.

Bricks and mortar retailers are having a tough go of it these days, and malls/shopping centers are seeing some of the most direct and painful outcomes of our economic malaise: nobody is shopping. What bodies are visible walking past stores are often just window-shopping, and more often than not the places are rather desolate, like a movie set for *I Am Legend*, or something.

Malls are the geophysical corollaries of the Internet, in that they bring stores together for easy access...only they can't do it as easily, conveniently, or economically. We saw most of them get a lot worse than Internet shopping this past holiday season, when merchandise was poorly displayed, thinly stocked, and badly served by few salespeople (fewer of whom had any desire to be stuck selling stuff in geophysical space).

So I guess the best Woodfield's branding can do is tell us that imaginary customers like to shop at its stores? I've thought about this a fair amount, have written and spoken on how retailers can make a go of it in this cyber-economy of ours. Here's a starter list of what Woodfield could consider:

- Stop relying on stores. Your tenants don't know how to drive traffic any more than you do. Just look at their numbers. It's nuts that you expect customers would come to your development because you have a list of tenants; they have too many options (how many of your retailers are truly one-of-a-kind?), including shopping online or, gasp, not shopping at all. You need to come to terms with the fact that you're responsible not just for nice brand awareness of your site – which, along with every other site in the known universe, is competing for dwindling consumer dollars – but that you need to drive behaviors that including buying stuff.

- Invent value-add benefits for the mall itself. Once you've written-off the stores, elevate your game, and come up with things that your mall can do for customers. Think gift-wrapping, only more, and more often (i.e. not just seasonal). Daycare for mommy shopping? Live events? A better system to help visitors find open parking spaces? Shopping bag storage? Impromptu rainy day promotions? The Americana at Brand (in CA) manages a frequent shopper points program, which incentivizes visits to the mall, and not just the stores within it. Remember, you're a destination, not just a real estate pad.

- You can't compete with the Internet. I know. It's cruel and unfair. But you need to stop thinking that your competition is the Internet, because you'll lose; instead, think about what you can do in geophysical, real space that the Internet can't match. For instance, Internet search can only tee-up items like a glorified checklist; you can work with your retailers to assemble meaningful, unique offers for your customers. Share business, and match retailers who target the same sort of real customers (instead of branding yourself with imaginary ones). Get them to realize that you all sink or swim together. Co-promote packages, bundles, experiences.

I think there's immense opportunity for developers to think differently about how they deliver brand difference, and there are good examples to copy. The Woodfield campaign isn't one of them.

(81) Amazon's Ad Contest

Amazon has announced a competition for customers to create their own 30-second video commercials for the brand. Two winners will each get $10,000 Amazon.com Gift Cards, and their work will be screened at "a U.S. film festival."

Forget for a moment that the whole point of a social media campaign like this isn't to create the ads themselves – in Amazon's case, it has never needed ads of any kind before, and isn't likely going to get particularly good ones from the crowd anyway – but rather to use the promotion to get the attention of a wider, non-UGC-creating audience.

So do you think anybody cares about it? The announcement got picked up in *PR-Inside.com*, the virtual ghost of the *Seattle PI*, and the leading source of the best ways to waste marketing dollars, *Brandweek*. As of last weekend, there were a whopping 13 posts in the company's forum on the topic.

I'm surprised that Amazon would do something so dull, but then again, it often does things that are really smart. While other businesses are "experimenting" with the conversational thing by prompting consumer conversations about conversing, Amazon has been quietly building dialogs based on its core function: recommending and selling books. Instead of running ads to make the usual brand promises, it has made its browsing and purchasing functionality just shy of perfect (at least compared to the messy, uneven experiences available at bricks-and-mortar retailers).

The branding we get from Amazon is all about doing things at the site, not trying to frame or describe them. It knows that the conversation aspect of business arises from the conduct of commerce, not parallel or separate from it. Its site isn't the most beautiful, but it simply works beautifully. This is directionally relevant knowledge for all brands, not just those that retail online.

Now, that doesn't mean that there aren't lots of opportunities for Amazon to do fun, engaging marketing. I can think of at least three ways it could have conducted a UGC ad contest that would have been far better grounded in the reality and strength of its brand:

1. Why not challenge reader communities to create ads for various genres? Get mystery fans to produce a spot, and sci-fi readers another. People usually feel strongly for their favorite sort of books, and are interested in sharing their obsessions with one another. The resulting commercials could be redundantly similar, or diverge so wildly in content and/or construction that they could come from different companies. Who'd care? The point would be to get lots of readers involved, and use that engagement to possible attract potential readers who might get drawn to the Amazon platform by a genre interest vs. a generic one.

2. Why use video and the outdated convention of a TV commercial? It's kind of like the early Ford Motor Co. hosting a competition for the best horse riding. Considering its aspirations for the Kindle, how about a UGC contest for every historic media distribution tool? Celebrate its digital book transmission with spots celebrating radio, kinescopes, daguerreotype photos, even print set by linotype? What about hand-drawn and decorated pages on vellum? This would position digital at the end of some historical path, and probably produce really interesting stuff. Make history the topic, not just personal expressions of the company's branding.

3. Wouldn't the cool challenge be to write something cool and compelling about a company that sells books? How about those genre fans collaborate on a crowdsourced short story or something? Conversely, it could be a competition to scribble "the perfect sentence." Think poetry, or a variety of written art forms. This UGC would be a lot easier to update and share, and lots more people could get involved. Why not allow every purchaser to contribute (or give shoppers a minimal discount if they pitch in)?

I suspect Amazon's ad contest is the result of them just not being good at doing this sort of nonsense, which is a credit to their business model. But that doesn't mean there aren't ways to make it work.

(82) Starbucks & Saks

As the economic meltdown continues to challenge our very premises about brands and selling, I'm intrigued to watch two well-known names respond to our dire circumstances in somewhat similar ways.

Starbucks is launching instant coffee: called *Via*, it promises to recreate the company's drinking experience at home or on the go, and for just a bit less than a hot small ("tall") cup of its coffee would cost in one of its outlets. Company execs say that the market is gigantic – 81% of coffee sales are instant – and company founder/chief reviver Howard Schultz says "this is a transformational event in the history of the company."

I just wonder if anybody wants to drink it.

Starbucks has always been more about the in-store experience than the actual coffee it served. Of course, the stuff had to be really good, but the brilliance of the concept was that the stores were a stop-over for drivers at which they got to encounter the smells, sights, and context of a coffee shop. The "third place" concept, while as old as the coffee houses of the Enlightenment, was new for harried commuters and unemployed consultants alike.

While confronted with serious price pressure for its high-margin kooky concoctions, Starbucks' real problem has been that its store experiences have become crowded and stinky. Too many people ordering too many customized drinks meant long waits, and it's just so plain irritating to listen to them order and complain. Adding cooked sandwiches to the menu meant odors of tuna and burnt bread wafted across you as you waited in line.

Does an instant coffee packet get consumers to engage with the Starbucks brand in some meaningful way? It sure saves them a visit to the stores, especially if the drinks are as tasty as promised. Transformational? Perhaps, but I would have expected lots of innovative, meaningful changes to the store experiences; other than a quickie 3-hour shut-down a while back to make sure employees had read their job description manuals, there's been not a word from Starbucks on changing the real drivers of its brand differentiation.

Saks Fifth Avenue seems to have a similar approach to avoiding those drivers of brand preference, in that its latest plans center on 1) reducing prices by selling cheaper stuff, and b) selling its real estate, if necessary.

It slashed prices as much as 75% during the holidays, so it has already revealed to its customers that what it used to charge was probably not warranted. Those price margins are never coming back. And once it rolls cheaper merchandise in its stores, it can try to differentiate itself from Target, Kohl's, and any of the other merchants who're chasing those newly-minted bargain consumers. Different displays? Better employees? New programs? Again, not a word.

Will cheap stuff be enough to make anybody want to shop there?

I just can't see how Saks can avoid focusing on its store experiences – and all of the benefits, services, add-ons, etc. that working with that context allows – and still hope to possess the stores a year or two from now. Maybe it wants its customers to shop online, which makes it an even tougher business to differentiate from every other online retailer?

But that sounds like instant department store packets to me.

(83) Andy Warhol's Branding Strategy

Back in the Dark Ages of the late 1960s, pop artist and Crispin Glover-inspiration Andy Warhol once quipped "in the future, everyone will be world-famous for fifteen minutes."

He meant fifteen seconds, right? Or perhaps the time it takes to post a shot on a social media site (and maybe add a single return volley)? Maybe it's however long a Super Bowl commercial might be? If Weathproof Garment Co. had its way, fame could be sliced into increments no longer than three seconds.

That's what the *Wall Street Journal* reported last week: Weatherproof had proposed to divvy up a 30-second spot with nine other brands, planning to give each about enough time to blurt out a company name.

Only guess what? A quick Internet search reveals that Weatherproof's PR impresario made the same announcement last year, duping mainstream reporters into covering it. The stunt was quickly exposed, generating lots of virtual press clippings as folks *tisk-tisked* the entire shebang. So is it news current, or past, or maybe never? Some more checking:

- The Weatherproof corporate site doesn't have a news report more current than one dated March 3, 2008.

- There's no publicly available list of the brands committed to blowing millions of dollars on Super Bowl XLIII.

- Most stories on the event focus on 1) how many big names have dropped out of the lavish expense, or 2) the ludicrous lengths marketers like GoDaddy will go to in order to get publicity for whatever they plan to do (or not).

Ah…make news with the *what if*, which prompts a snippet of time far beyond whatever could get bought by a commercial. Who cares what, how, or why? Remember, Warhol repeated his 15 seconds-quip for the next few decades, achieving repeat recognition simply because he was recognized repeatedly. It would be tough to find a better, more pure and unadulterated example of the utter inanity of traditional brand thinking:

- Exposure for exposure's sake.

- Distraction in the name of awareness.

- Attitudinal attributions and associations that exist for nothing more than, quite literally, the blink of an eye (or jab in an online forum).

Andy Warhol branding strategy. Don't blink, or you might miss it.

Just For Fun: Give Us A Hit

David Byrne, the erstwhile leader of the late-70s+ new wave band Talking Heads, has created an art installation in London in which visitors can pound on an archaic organ keyboard and make the walls and beams of a railway shed vibrate, clank, and shudder.

He's a marketing genius, but I'm not all that fond of his music. I think he's bored, and this latest project sounds really boring (pun intended).

Like writing, painting, and acting, the best, most engaging musical creations twist, bend, and invert or extend the conventions of structure and form. It's easy to blow stuff up, or ignore (or simply not know) the basics of grammar, a color wheel, or the rigors of script memorization.

Ultimately, art needs to conform to some sensory purpose. Writing needs to be read...paintings seen, acting witnessed, and music heard. And it needs to be enjoyed. Without explanation of importance, or a detailed argument for why something is good. Therefore, I'd argue that revolutions occur within these constraints, or at least they're enabled by them.

Talking Heads did just that with its music; it was consciously arty, and there was an entire backstory that you could care about it you chose. But it *rocked*, and it was easy to dance to (in deference to *American Bandstand*), like popular music is supposed be.

Byrne's following projects were also well within the context of musical expectation, even as they poked and pushed lots of boundaries. His sampling drone-thing with Brian Eno – *My Life in the Bush of Ghosts* – was absolutely brilliant. He wrote music for Twyla Tharp's dance *The Catherine Wheel*, which sounded kind of like *Talking Heads* and the Eno collaboration all mashed together (I loved it, too).

Then he ran out of room in the rock idiom.

Sure, he's since dabbled in Brazilian ethnic music, and the requisite pairings with young hip hop artists. It's all fine and good, but it's nothing revolutionary. It's not even *evolutionary*, but oddly static. Irrelevant. Popular music is no less a structured format than, say, Gregorian chants; when the music isn't catchy or different enough to be popular, it's just *bad*.

So now he's playing a building.

I'm sure there'll be some people who fall to their knees because of the auditory magic of the experience. Art, like all communication, is a subjective experience, and there's no denying that at least some listeners will love what they hear. But the idea of a physical structure making sounds isn't the same as making music. Wind chimes have been doing it for many centuries, and any building squeaks and rings on a blustery day.

This is where Byrne's marketing brilliance comes into play.

"You can't play Bach," he says, "[so] it kind of levels the playing field as far as performance goes. We are all equally amateur at it. It's supposed to be accessible to ordinary folks." These comments get him written up in main-stream media as a visionary and daring artiste, and all but guarantees that there'll be bodies walking through his exhibit.

I think the video game *Guitar Hero* makes music a lot more accessible to ordinary folks. Wouldn't it be more interesting if extraordinary folks like Byrne could find a novel, engaging way to make music sound novel and engaging, like:

- Write a pop song that's at once familiar and yet utterly new.

- Bring an unexpected, incongruous element to a dance song, so it simultaneously moves people to shake their bodies as it blows their minds.

- Byrne could mine his *Talking Heads* catalog and somehow refashion it into something entirely different, yet recognizable enough to let us enjoy it.

This art installation thing just seems so empty, so artistically unchallenging. Giving us a hit would be the real challenge, both for Byrne's musical abilities, and his marketing acumen.

Chapter Nine
Radical Action Plans

Did you know that I volunteered to be a board member of GM?

I know, it was a selfless act of patriotism, not just a businessman's largesse. I even went to the trouble of writing a strategic brief on what I'd do for the company:

- Help marketing refocus on prompting more marketshare instead of mindshare.

- Get operations contributing and participating in the ongoing dialog with the public.

- Explore innovative ways to differentiate the GM offering, like looking to finance and service as ways to augment the sometimes ephemeral promises of branding.

I was generally willing to do whatever radical action it might take, irrespective of ownership or reward, to get GM back on its feet. Only I didn't get a reply. Well, I addressed a blog post to the headhunters who were trying to fill the jobs, so maybe they never saw it.

My radical ideas weren't the only ones to get overlooked, though. For all of the talk about "innovation" and experimentation, 2009 was just as notable for its risk-avoidance. Partly a function of difficult economic times, I think businesses also found it hard to translate into coherent action the calls to throw various rule-books out the window. Marketing seemed particularly resistant to those challenges: for every dare to be new, digital, or just radically different, the ensuing programs still pretty much looked and functioned like always.

The real opportunities then, and now, were to see past the conventions of tradition, and even proven experience, and experiment cross-departmentally, across multiple consumer groups, and with varied combinations of corporate partnerships. Looking at old challenges in truly new ways requires radical actions plans, only there weren't many to report during the year.

Here's another personal example: When I had a problem with my iPhone, my calls to the brands involved in providing the product's functionality resulted in no action. All they did was confirm that their contribution to the product worked just fine. Nobody owned the problem. So I wrote a magazine column about the utility of a joint-service arrangement, especially for complex technology products coming from multi-company partnerships. I asked, wouldn't it be smarter marketing to spend less on ads, and instead create a real, single-source service benefit for customers?

After my article appeared, these businesses all emailed me…offering more help, but nobody could address, let alone consider, my service idea. Granted, there are probably a million reasons why my solution didn't fit into the standard business practices behind my phone, but the story might be emblematic of how companies in general are not yet ready to explore the radical answers that today's questions demand.

"Radical" things don't quite fit neatly into planning models, yet I think it's one of the ideas that you'll need to explore going forward.

Even though I may not be joining the GM board anytime soon, it didn't stop me from offering my expertise for a number of other businesses during the year. I like writing about "radical" opportunities. So I've collected the best essays on how well-known companies could pursue novel, if not outright radical, strategies to succeed in the marketplace:

(84) Speaking With One Voice

My essay last week in *Information Week* about my difficulties getting a single answer from the companies partnered behind my iPhone generated one basic response from readers of my post: *Duh.*

OK, the actual responses were a bit different, but were more like three variations on a theme:

1. I'm dumb, and I should do a better job of solving my own technology issues.

2. The iPhone is dumb, so I should pick a different product to own (see first response).

3. Such a situation is dumb and all too common (see first and second responses).

It was that third conclusion that compelled me to write the post in the first place. My problem – a quirky inability to send emails a second time after having done so quite easily the first – had proved insolvable by the three technology partners responsible for my iPhone experience. Apple, AT&T, and GoDaddy had each been very pleasantly unhelpful on the phone, and their various forums (and third-party resources) had given me no useful answers.

What they'd each done is confirm that their parts of the integrated whole were functioning just fine.

So I'd written that this was downright silly. It was as if I had a medical problem, but my options were only to visit a series of specialists without having access to a general practitioner. From a branding perspective, wasn't this a significant liability for each of the participants in the partnership (or so I mused), as consumers expect products and services to work, irrespective of who is responsible for what aspect of that performance?

I felt that this might be a major stumbling block for technology brands facing a future wherein more of what they sell will be integrated with things that other brands are selling. As a consumer, I don't want to know that Apple's hardware is working fine, per se, any more than I would want confirmation from the coolant manufacturer that my fridge Freon was charged even though my milk was turning to cottage cheese.

Thinking as a marketer, I wanted to know why there wasn't more time/money spent up front on providing truly integrated, component-agnostic support, and whether that was a smart go-forward branding premise.

Here I was thinking that a major branding threshold for technology providers was to offer seamlessly integrated stuff, like appliances, and two-thirds of my responders felt the exact opposite: it was my responsibility to be the integrator, and there's nothing wrong with that (just something wrong with me). I got a fair number of very well-intentioned suggestions on what specifically I might try. A chunk of them were unimpressed with my branding conclusions, and said I should pick another product.

Now granted, *Information Week* readers are a technology-savvy, insider group, and their reactions weren't illustrative of how the general consumer might feel. So I ask you:

- Shouldn't there be unified, one-stop destinations for support for services or devices that involve multiple partners? At a minimum, shouldn't customer support quantify and qualify the "top ten" problems that each partner encounters, and cross-reference them in a formal, thoughtful way, so you can find solutions more easily?

- Would this help or hurt the participating brands (or have no impact either way)?

- Is such an offering something that you'd pay for, on top of the normal service that comes with the purchase (or lack thereof)?

I should add that my essay prompted contact from high-level people at both AT&T and GoDaddy, and that they were very thoughtful and earnest in trying to fix my specific problem. I'm thankful for it.

Thinking again as a marketer, though, it's intriguing that I got said calls as a result of my posting (one of the folks actually monitors Twitter), and not simply as a regular customer. My problem wasn't a social media issue, but simply a service problem. And I wasn't fishing for help, but rather using my woes to suggest a business strategy opportunity.

If those brands spoke with one voice the first time I encountered a problem with my *iPhone*, I would have been a far happier customer...and written a post illustrating a business success case history, not a still-undelivered promise.

(85) My Plan for Skype

Now that eBay has put *Skype* up for sale, it's an intriguing question to ponder whether an IPO or acquisition makes the most sense. I think a better question would be to reconsider what's going on.

Skype is a poster child for how successful, and misleading, technology hype can be.

It was the brainchild of the folks who gave the world KaZaA, which was a fast-follower P2P file sharing application right after Napster created and broadened the marketplace for illegally swapping media files (Napster was shut down in 2001). Calling the demand for such services a "marketplace" is a bit wobbly, as nobody was paying for any of it, so there was no actual market. The brilliance of KaZaA was that it got gobs of people to do something for free, required no effort, and had no real-world consequences.

Sound familiar?

The founders went on to invent *Skype*, which was conceived as a KaZaA-like P2P app for swapping voice. Utilizing Voice over Internet Protocol (VoIP), it was able to let people use their computers like phones and, better yet, do it for free. It had 100 million registered users within its first 3 years of operation, which helped inspire eBay to pay $2.6 billion for it. And then eBay promptly forgot about it.

I guess the rationale, if there ever was one beyond the giddy nonsense of "we'll figure out how to monetize it later on," was to let eBay's customers use Skype as a tool to communicate with one another. But I couldn't find a Skype icon anywhere on eBay this morning, and it's not even offered as a way to contact eBay customer service.

When eBay's boss claims that "…separating *Skype* will allow eBay to focus entirely on our two core growth strategies…" I don't think he's being terribly honest. eBay has spent no obvious time, nor made any significant public gestures, evidencing even the slightest focus on Skype. Similarly, Skype has introduced some services of its own (like calling out to real phones), and grew revenue to $145 in 4Q08, but continues to operate and appear as a spunky, inconsistently reliable, free-standing start-up.

(Disclosure: I use Skype occasionally. My name is "baskinjs").

So what's going on? Well, I think Skype is a perfect candidate for a dim bulb plan, so here's the skinny:

- VoIP is cool. With the advent of ubiquitous hot spots, and various technologies (like 3G) to get Internet stuff on mobile devices without having the wait for the paint to dry, means that there's a viable network on which to conduct conversations (and any other data transactions).

- VoIP is cheap. It'll always cost less than a proprietary network. Being generic is also a drawback, as Skype (or any VoIP provider) is trying to make money offering bathers voluntary help stepping into a free ocean.

- VoIP isn't a business. Put aside all the poetic blather about networks and systems and glorious misrepresentations of reality found in slide presentations. The only reason Skype was worth anything a few years ago was because the context around it was nuts. Remember, eBay wrote off pretty much all the price it paid for it only a few years later. Can anyone say "bubble hangover?"

- Skype is a community. Forget for a moment all of the entertainment-based communities we normally celebrate, like Facebook and You-Tube. People use Skype for a specific, purposeful reason: to talk to one another. So it has a real-world utility, by definition and, accordingly, its users have something in common other than a shared interest in Susan Boyle's singing debut. Further, the very use of Skype creates and supports community; it enables communities every time people reach out to one another.

- Skype is a service. Well, it doesn't understand that, but it is. The service available to users now is embarrassingly inadequate (i.e. there is none). Skype operates as a technology, and it's supported as one, with all the requisite FAQs and outsourced responsibilities. But with 370 million registered users, and nearly 8% of the world's total voice minutes originating with it, you'd think it would be something more (see Community above)?

- Skype needs a purpose. Or purposes. Big, bold, hairy ones the "change the world," or "being the best voice app in existence," and offering the service to support it. Donating x% of every call to fighting global warming, so users become true eco-warriors. Becoming the only viable alternative to business travel. Establishing real communities of users (around geography, topic, or interest), so that each use is a dip into community, and the communities get smarter, more relevant, and bigger. Or all of the above.

Figuring out how to make money giving something away for free is a crappy business model, all of the happy new media prognosticating aside. Skype has zillions of users with at least something meaningful in common. Its strategy should be based on defining purposes, not just technology, services, or even the faux appearance of community that's so in vogue these days.

This would raise really intriguing options for an IPO or acquisition, wouldn't it? I'd love to help write that offering prospectus for a newly-envisioned Skype, based on the promise of tangible user interests. You can just imagine how boring the plan for the business as currently configured would look by comparison. Potential acquirers could be businesses that need to establish (or attach) purpose-driven communities to their brands. So it's not just telecos in the bidding anymore. Think oil company. Commodity consumer product, like Coke. Maybe a CE product manufacturer or, even Microsoft.

None of these opportunities will ever see the light of day unless the management at eBay and Skype come to terms with what's really going on. No dim bulb is bright enough to illuminate it for them.

(86) Car Companies as Mutual Funds

I had a chance to present to members of the Luxury Marketing Council of Southern California a few weeks ago, and they challenged my thinking – and got me thinking – about how to apply a "brand is behavior" approach to selling autos coming out of Detroit.

One of the prompts was a simple question: "What could Cadillac to get me to forsake replacing my Acura RL with another one two years from now, and buy domestic instead?" Another participant commented "Will the Chevy Volt be a success, considering both the wait (two years or more), and likely price point of $40,000 or more?"

I had to think about things a bit more before I could formulate a reasonable response. And then it hit me: There's nothing that the traditional branding and marketing playbook can offer Detroit. If the next round of vehicles is churned through the same communications machine that last year burned through $6 billion, the companies are doomed. There's just not enough time to effect the incremental change in consumer buying habits; remember, the switchover to Asian imports took decades, not years. And that would presume that the marketers could invent marketing that actually worked.

Further, there's just not enough variability in the metal and functions of the vehicles to build a case for differentiation. More and more, cars are tending to resemble one another, perform like one another, and last about the same amount of time. Sure, there are differences, and some of them are very nuanced, but I don't think that claims of a smooth ride or handy cup-holders carry the legitimacy that they once did. Service offers and promotional prices are effectively generic.

Add on top of it all the fact that credit is still tight, and people are feeling financially strapped, so there are some serious externalities affecting Detroit's ability to sell cars, even if people want to buy them. Marketing can't overcome these problems. But I think a radically new business strategy might do it.

I think the Detroit automakers should function as if they were mutual funds.

Instead of buying or leasing a hunk of metal, consumers would buy a share or portion of the company; they'd literally "buy into" the idea that these companies matter, and can provide goods and services that other people would want to buy. Actual vehicles and service coverage would "cost" some level(s) of investment in the company; you could buy a portion of a future vehicle, and hope that the value of your investment would increase over time. More importantly, this set-up would create a number of positive, shared incentives:

- For starters, the value of your shares would go up if other people bought in, so there'd be a real incentive to evangelize for your company.

- As a shareholder, you'd take a more serious interest in how the vehicles were manufactured and distributed, which would provide the basis for lots of social media interaction and collaboration (instead of chat about whether or not you like the ads).

- Shareholders would vest more fully over time, providing a growing and powerful incentive to both stay engaged, and be a loyal buyer. Imagine frequent driver points as an added benefit.

I have no idea how it would be structured, or whether it would even work. But it would focus "ownership" on the company and its products in a tangible, involving way unlike stock ownership.

Imagine if the U.S. government didn't give the bailout money directly to the automakers, but instead handed Americans checks, and told them to make an investment in one or more of the companies? Talk about building accountability into the disbursement. And maybe it would be a business strategy that actually had a chance of working?

(87) My Recovery Plan For Twitter

I wrote recently about how odd it is that we regular folks think we're smarter, more capable, and certainly more honest than the leaders of real-world businesses, like carmakers and financial institutions, yet we blithely defer to the machinations of technology leaders...even when we don't know what their plans might be.

Such was the situation Friday when Twitter received $35 million in additional funding from International Venture Partners and Benchmark. The company said that it hadn't been looking for the money, but the offer was just too good to pass up.

Twitter has never made a dime, by the way. It has attracted legions of consumers for its free service, but then again, so has the atmosphere; like breathing, there's no reasonable expectation that doing so is ever going to make money. There's just hope, and trust, in the myth of the boy-genius technology entrepreneur: the founders promise to emerge in short-order, and reveal to the Universe their brilliant plans, which will defy history, economics, and sundry laws of causality.

It's funny that we demand that GM's leadership spell out its plans to sell cars in excruciatingly painful and humiliating detail, and only then grudgingly give it a dime. But the technology wiz-kid fantasy du jour? There's somebody willing to hand them $35 million, which should have been even harder to get than public largesse. GM is going to embarrass everyone, but Twitter will make its investors proud. They just *know* it.

Whether admitted or not, lots of private capital investing is based on Black Swan theory, which is just shy of outright gambling. Money isn't spent because of the certitude of a company striking gold; it's invested on the bet that a business idea will defy the very conventions that make it such a risk, and on how surprising, and surprisingly huge, such breakthroughs usually are.

Twitter isn't getting money because it's a sure bet, but rather because it's such a long-shot. So I want to invest my two cents to help it succeed: here is my Three Point Plan to help it defy those odds, confound the critics, and become a recurring game-changer:

1. Step out of the conference room. Let's face it, the smarty-pants *technoentrepeneur myth* is just a myth: just because one college-aged guy chanced on something that caught on doesn't make him smarter than the thousands of similarly-talented innovators whose ideas were either too early, too late, or just didn't quite fit like his did. So when you or any other wiz-kids retreat into your echo chamber bubbles, it satisfies and reinforces your sense of self-aggrandized worth, but it doesn't bode well for future breakthroughs. It's just the wrong set-up (see Bill Gates). The first step in finding that next breakthrough is to step out of the conference room (or private jet) and try to replicate the circumstances from which breakthroughs emerge. I have no idea what those criteria were when you dreamt up Twitter, but I bet they included being in touch with lots of other, real people, and understanding (perhaps intuitively) what they like and want to do. Not via focus groups, or from those other brilliant investor-types who populate your board. For real.

2. Give up the next innovation to your users. Forget plotting the money-making ideas that you'll dump on them, and let them co-invent the next steps. Treat the community like a real community, and build the development conversation into the fabric of tweets, putting a simple question to users: we need to monetize this service, so what would that mean to you? By definition, all of the ideas from digital agencies intended to exploit said users would be rejected, as would probably most other actions that would overly-*crapify* the interface (see MySpace for details). It might also create a sense of ownership and involvement heretofore unimagined by the experts at Twitter World HQ. Think less corporate genius, and more public radio.

3. You need to create a platform for constant change, not ideas to make money. Whatever gets invented over the next 12 months at Twitter, there'll be all those other brilliant wiz-kids busy working to invent better stuff. Competition is constant, and the siren call of other fads, especially free ones, will constantly lure folks away from your platform, and VC money is like buying love. It's not sustainable. So once you get users co-inventing and managing their Twitter experience, you have to create ways to institutionalize that innovation. Less consumers, and more citizens. Could Twitter users vote on new ideas? Are there milestones for introducing radical new services and tools, so everyone knows that everything will change so-and-so often? If Twitter isn't fundamentally different a year from now, it'll be distant history. And adding ads and other garbage doesn't count.

I doubt we'll see any of this from Twitter, of course, and we'll get far too detailed (and unreliable) plans from GM and Chrysler. All of these companies are beholden to outdated processes and expectations, even if some of them are in businesses that look and feel really futuristic.

Twitter probably doesn't need to fix something that's not broken. Until it breaks.

(88) Trendy Is As Trendy Does

Apparel retailer marketing is usually pretty nutty, and these businesses are on the bleeding edge of consumer spending trends. I'm fascinated that JCPenney will focus its spring advertising on bargain-priced items from trendy designers like Kimora Lee Simmons and Nicole Miller.

Trends are capricious, by definition, and they're also exclusionary (for something to be trendy, something else must not be) and impermanent (if it's not current, then it's not a trend...it's history). In fashion apparel, these qualities are at hyper-speed, with the volume turned all the way up to 11. It's a killer market that comes with the near-certain guarantee that even the winners will ultimately lose one day, and likely fail as big as they once succeeded.

So why would JCPenney elect to base its advertising (and thus its branding, as far as this dim bulb can figure) on a small selection of avowedly trendy merchandise?

I suspect that the intention is to break through the clutter. Trendy clothes, especially from a brand name like JCPenney, might prompt that cognitive dissonance that we otherwise refer to as buzz. Consumers might think about JCPenney, and do so in a different way. Combined with the budget-pricing, it might tell would-be luxury buyers (or aspirational ones) that they can get famously trendy stuff for less at JCPenney.

This strategy presumes that anybody *needs* the stuff, which they don't.

The bigger trend that will matter for the foreseeable future is that consumers don't think they have money to spend. Many actually don't have it. Sure, people have loads of wants – fantasies and wish lists thrived in the last Great Depression – but their purchase decisions are dictated in large part by necessities, not desires. The challenge is to invent ways that translate products and services – however luxurious, trendy, or otherwise unnecessary – into those necessary purchases.

I don't think JC Penney is going to accomplish it by offering exorbitantly priced brand names with less-rapacious price-tags. A rip-off is a rip-off or, more fairly to the company, a want isn't a need.

What could the company do differently, and really deliver a compelling, need-prompting brand strategy? It would have to involve its operational departments far beyond the purview of marketing and its seemingly forever-replenished kitty:

- New employment structure. Why not come up with novel programs to employ more people (less hours/more services?), thereby inviting the community into the store to help it and themselves succeed? Where's the "work here/buy here" program that encourages families to shop and invite neighbors to do so, too, thereby receiving discounts and/or other benefits?

- Trend subscriptions. If trendy clothing is designed to appear dated after a season, why couldn't parents subscribe to a clothing program that got teens into the latest fashion and then, at the end of a period, involved some return/exchange for the next season's fashion (and some community donation/give-back)? Let consumers amortize clothing expenses (or other expenditures) over time via something other than an onerous credit card balance.

- Turn stores into community centers. Why not apply a radical new approach to the role of stores in the communities they serve, and open them to meetings, art exhibits, musical events, etc.? Each event would be a draw to would-be shoppers, and they could see that a side-effect of their patronage would be fed back into their cities and towns.

Perhaps the strategy would be to skip the latest trends of fashion, and redefine the Penney brand in terms that were tangible, real, and sustainable. It wouldn't be sexy, but it might very well be profitable and sustainable.

(89) Best Buy's Dire Prophecy

Best Buy announced last week that its sales this quarter are down sharply, and that things don't look any better for the rest of the year. The news came with the requisite promises of "adjustments" to inventory and spending from the finance department. Aside from an oblique reference to "gaining market share," marketing was pretty much silent, which is also typical of these types of announcements.

For a news event, there really wasn't much news involved. The crappy economy has been the cause and/or effect cited in most media stories for the past few months. It would have been surprising had Best Buy said anything positive, as the regulatory obligation and smart business strategy was to lower expectations.

Couldn't it have used the occasion to talk about its brand in terms that would have been relevant to its customers? With the implicit promise that sales would stink, it could have declared that it would:

- Improve customer service. The differences between flat screen TV's remain incomprehensible to most people. Folks are cautious about making the wrong purchase even in flush times. Lots of gizmos require integration with services or other gizmos. Imagine doing lots of intensive associate training, incentives, and back-end support to turn customer service into a strategic customer differentiator (and poacher).

- Launch unique refurb/service offerings. If people aren't buying, then add dimensions to the offering so you give me other/better reasons to visit the store. Where's the "upgrade your PC" bundle? How about something that lets people make existing products work (or look) better? Maybe add some long-term, back-end services deal to the price on new devices, like an automaker extending its drive-train warranty?

- Experiment. If it's proving hard to drive consumers into stores, it's time to go nuts with innovative ways to work around the problem. How about the aggressive deals to get every vendor, supplier, partner, and associate family member into the stores? Or a social media promo that awards a $500 gift certificate every day (or every hour) through the end of the year? Why couldn't strange, blue light special-like things occur in-store, so there's a reason why you want to be walking around one?

The "You, Happier" ads are nice, but they're not motivational in a "get off your butt and into the stores" sort of way. They're almost too nice, promoting vague feelings in a very typical effort to associate the brand with lifestyle. We already know what our "lifestyles" are going to be this holiday season... impoverished, or afraid of being so.

So these spots pretty much attest to the premise that the company expects its prophecy to come true.

It could just as easily refuse to go silently into the night, and take the market externalities as an outright dare...not to just suffer, but reaffirm and reinvent its business. That's radical, pure branding upside, isn't it?

I don't know what the marketing would look like, and it's way too late to start making noises about challenging the Status Quo. But if they'd asked me, I would have suggested that Best Buy use this dire sales circumstance to establish better, closer, and more aggressively satisfying relationships with its customers. And that it should tell everyone about it.

Then, maybe the prophecy wouldn't be so dire after all.

(90) Holiday Insurance

In our era of heightened expectations and outsourced responsibilities, I'm surprised that we aren't able to insure holidays.

A single family get-together – say, for Christmas tomorrow – adds up to an apparent endless number of interconnected variables. Change one, and some and/or all of the others are affected. Weather, guest health, personalities, mood, food quality, presents, order of presents given, music, conversation topics, you name it. Our mental pictures of a happy holiday are idealized and usually static, while our experience is dynamic and multi-dimensional. And thus full of risks.

So why can't we insure them?

I mean, I don't want to simply *hope* for a nice holiday event, or wish it had been more satisfying after-the-fact. And it's not like I'm ever going to be surprised by what happens, at least not completely, and certainly not if it's at an annual holiday shindig. Past events and behaviors already give me a range of possibilities, or identify the variables that might most impact the gig.

It shouldn't be surprising that no snow on Christmas might make everyone's mood slightly less cheery, or that too much might ruin things, too. There's a solid chance that my kid will find that electronic gizmo X wasn't the be-all/end-all gift she claimed it was on her wish list. Uncle Fred (or someone else) could arrive with a head cold, and the chicken might get overcooked. Some younger cousin will enrage an older one, whether by declaring affection for anarchism, or simply refusing to answer questions in anything longer than grunts.

But if I can list these variables, why couldn't I assign values to them – likelihood, casual links, the "cost" of resulting outcomes – and insure myself? I'm thinking three-levels of holiday insurance:

1. Pre-event planning services. If some outside agency could help me identify and assign values to my event variables, it might also assist with planning to avoid or overcome the negative ones (and encourage and expand the good ones). I'm too busy worrying about getting the card-chairs from the basement to think about how unpleasant cousin Daphne will be for the entire evening if she hits her head on the doorway, like she did a few years ago. It would be great for some service to make a note of it, and give me a preparatory solution that let me (and my guests) reduce the risk of that variable to zero. Ditto for seating arrangements, trade-offs between what I cook vs. what I buy pre-made, and whether the field of Republican hopefuls can be safely discussed at all.

2. Real-time event support. One of the hardest aspects of any holiday gig is that once it's happening, there's usually nothing you can do

about it. The event simply unfolds, or unravels, and all you can do is ride the wave and hope you don't drown. When the appetizer singes, a friend of the family drinks too much, or the guitar for the video game my kid wanted only works once before going silent, there's no customer service to call for immediate assistance. What if I could call some real-time support line, kind of like an event concierge, who could get things done while getting them done still mattered to the quality of the experience? Need more ice delivered? A homemade fix for radio game controllers? A new conversation topic for your niece who is sitting in the corner staring strangely at ornaments? Maybe there are a set of event health indicators – number of arguments about God, sidelong references about how small my house is, percentage of food left untouched on napkins and plates, or gallons alcohol consumed – that a service tracks in real time, and proactively offers advice before they lead to irrevocable changes to the party?

3. Post-event payoff. Sometimes, planning an annual holiday event is like getting ready for a hurricane or earthquake; you can try to minimize the damage, but the thing is going to hit pretty much not matter what. If I can insure my roof or basement from damage, why can't I insure my party? If an argument is bound to happen, or the beans will likely come out cold even after repeated irradiation in the microwave, it would be nice to get some monetary recompense the next day, just to soothe my jagged nerves. Assessing the cost, and then finding the investor parties interested in assuming such risks, would be far less dicey than spinning those cute-rate, never-going-to-get-paid home mortgages, wouldn't it? Maybe a post-party user assessment would canvas all party-goers, and come up with a conclusion review that triggered payoff not just to the host, but to everyone involved. We could all be "insured" from the possibility of having a bad time.

We can already insure our physical existence, and things like vacation travel commitments. It isn't such a stretch from insuring the material aspects of life, to insuring our ephemeral life experiences, is it? Think holidays, secular events, even daily routines (imagine being able to insure your average weekday). The services and technology development opportunities might be immense. It would also make the brand marketing a lot easier, if not simply a lot more fun.

Who needs to get consumers to engage with cavemen or bulldog mascots when you can promise them great life experiences?

(91) MyPlan for MySpace

MySpace has fired 30% of its workforce, or about 400 people, just as parent company News Corp. scrapped a $350 million plan to consolidate it in a new office with the other components of Fox Interactive Media.

Most of the business coverage sites blame falling advertising sales and traffic gains by Facebook. As you may know, News Corp. is busy implementing a strategic overhaul to combat these two issues, having recruited a new CEO for all its digital operations from AOL (an expert in falling ad sales), and one for MySpace from Facebook (adept at prompting visits that make it no money). Think about this for a minute:

- AOL tumbled from a valuation of $164 billion when it was bought in the 1990s by Time Warner, to something under $6 billion today (TW is trying to dump it).

- In the meantime, services like Facebook and Twitter have captured an inordinate amount of consumers' time: Facebook users in the U.S. alone chalked up 13.9 billion minutes on the site in April, 2009, while the nearly 300 minutes on Twitter were an increase of 3,712% over the same period last year.

- Facebook and Twitter haven't yet figured out how to make money. Twitter's founders have said they don't even care to try.

So MySpace is failing to make money competing with companies that give stuff away for free? Talk about a thankless proposition.

I've got to say that Rupert Murdoch deserves a lot of credit for taking it on. It's scary that trying to make money is such an exceptional idea. Doesn't anybody remember the Dot Com Bubble? I bet it must drive Murdoch nuts that none of the business media coverage, nor expert [sic] analysis, ever points out the dichotomy of a for-profit endeavor competing in an industry that isn't really an industry, but more of a free lunch. What are they competing on, favorable media clips?

Maybe MySpace shouldn't look to said "industry" for ideas on what to do...any more than it should have looked to the archaic business of ad placement as a way to accomplish anything more than muck up its U/I. Here's what it might consider instead:

- Find a purpose. Lose the "a place for friends" tagline. It's like subheading Ford with "vehicles for driving," or "Chicago, a place with buildings." Then, define a purpose for the space, or series of purposes. Think something between a political campaign and a video game: the site's foundation in music might be a good place to start. Dare to declare it, like "we're going to find a million bands" or "listen to endless music," or whatever.

- Build a real community. The latest reports on bloggers and Twitter users who create content for social media are far less than inspiring, and Facebook's lackluster user turnout to vote on a major structural change suggests that 1) most users are watchers, and 2) their presence is less about being in a community, and more like sitting in front of a TV watching *Gilligan's Island*. A purpose for MySpace could be the prompt for visitors to actually do things that are unique and/or exclusive to the site. Make membership mean something.

- Nix the exploitation. Stop the presses...MySpace isn't an ad channel, it's a place where people do things (check old tagline for a hint). The opportunity is to monetize their behavior, not try to distract from it with advertising. If the site were a place that people did things that had a purpose, you might actually be able to make those activities profitable. The flip side would be an opportunity to clean up all the ads that currently clutter the site.

I know I'm just throwing out the thoughts of a dim bulb, and the details behind my three bullet points would be many and complex. But the bright bulbs haven't really produced such shining results, have they?

(92) The Abandoned Tollbooth

Time Warner is going to spin off AOL by the end of the year. It should hurry up.

It paid $124 billion in 2001; while that's less than a decade ago, it might has well have been a different planet. Back then, the Internet was fast becoming the superhighway for business and entertainment, and AOL owned one of the first and largest tollbooths. It was the Google and Twitter of its day. AOL made money, and seemed poised to be perhaps the dominant portal for Internet experience. Some critics even worried that it was poised to take over the Internet.

Then the portal model disappeared, along with all the excitingly vague promises that constituted the .com bubble. Oh, and AOL operated mostly on dial-up phone lines, which is kind of like owning a buggy whip distributorship. Subscribers and traffic have fallen ever since, from 25+ million paying users to just under 7 million subscribers at the end of last year (it lost over a half million in the first quarter of 2009 alone). Ad revenue dropped 20% in the first quarter, after dropping 18% in 4Q2008. It still commands the fourth largest online audience in the U.S., though, and it earns a profit from pushing ads in front of all those eyeballs, even if said eyeballs don't belong to the youngest, hippest, or most likely to spend.

The problem is that sucking the Internet through the digital corollary of a McDonald's straw doesn't have a future. Time Warner's $6 billionish stake values the access and ad businesses as roughly equivalent, but I'd suspect those dial-ups go away faster than it would hope (and don't represent the right eyeballs for advertisers to exploit anyway).

So what happens differently for a stand-alone AOL? First and foremost, Time Warner can forget about it. That's a huge accomplishment, kind of like Daimler Benz dumping Chrysler on Cerberus. hen, after you wade past all the nonsense blather about "renewed focus" and whatever else the marketers make up to explain how getting abandoned at 5% of its original value is a good thing, you get to CEO Armstrong's strategy: Content.

It's an old media approach, really. Armstrong wants to rebuild the tollbooth to the Internet highway, only with a brick wall after the coin bucket. A really pretty wall, but a wall nevertheless, on which will be lots of ads.

AOL has all this traffic, even if it's shrinking, so it sees its challenge as that of monetizing those visits with advertising revenue. TMZ, AOL News, Asylum, and lots of sites on the drawing boards will give folks reasons to stay at AOL-owned properties, commercial access to which it can sell to the highest bidders.

I think this strategy has two problems: first, the ad model for Internet visits is going to fade away much like the portal idea did. Nobody likes online ads, and their ROI efficacy still befuddles otherwise smart marketers. Second, there's nothing saying that AOL can develop content any better than, well, anybody else. That's why broadcast and cable TV networks outsource program development to the marketplace, as do the movie makers in Hollywood. It's like AOL owns an empty warehouse and wants to compete with a fine arts museum by painting its own pictures, and then displaying them with ads.

All is not lost, of course. AOL could choose to invent real, behavioral ways to impact the lives of its visitors:

- I've never understood why it hasn't built real communities, not just the easy, anonymous throwaway traffic of chat.

- Ditto for its thriving email business, which could provide platforms for communities and/or outsourced corporate networks.

- Why couldn't visiting the Internet through AOL be some badge or tool to do so better, faster, or more intelligently?

- Being an AOL member could have a frequent-troller loyalty component, irrespective of what sites get visited.

- Where's the AOL social search bar?

Without such true invention, not just the blather about "innovation," I worry that Time Warner is simply abandoning a tollbooth that'll take us nowhere. If so, it should drive away as quickly as possible.

(93) Memo to Blockbuster's Agency

To: Bob Chimbel, DDB Entertainment

cc: All Innovative Ad Execs Throughout the Cosmos

Congratulations on winning the Blockbuster account, and on using it as the prompt to pull together all of your far-flung entertainment-related units into a single shop-within-Omnicom in Dallas. I understand that your client's CEO plans to transform the Blockbuster brand "into an entertainment provider" just like Apple did for its business. He has been working to evolve from a video-rental chain to a full-service media delivery company, according to the article I read in *Advertising Age*.

Somebody needs to tell you that the strategy is doomed. Even if it weren't, you're not the right guys to deliver it.

Sorry, I mean no insult to your skills. It's just that the mandate reflects a fundamental misunderstanding of what's going on the marketplace, and it promises to misapply your marketing skills to challenges that not even the most brilliant, innovative marketers could overcome. I see three primary issues:

1. The world needs another media delivery company like it needs a hole in the head. I don't care if the brand names are originally analog (Time/Warner, *Wall Street Journal*) or digital inventions (name the failed portal of your choice), the online distribution business is more a wireless-and-pipes play than anything else. What could Blockbuster possibly bring to this marketplace that Comcast, Amazon, YouTube,

or any number of other entrants don't already offer (or, worse, have tried and discarded)?

2. Blockbuster is a store, not a brand name, and certainly not an entertainment provider. To even suggest otherwise is to reveal a misplaced belief in the (your) ability to overcome reality, and convince people of things that are simply not true. There's no Blockbuster without the geophysical stores and physical merchandise. That's why the comparisons to Apple are incorrect: Apple sells hardware, and wraps an enabling service around it. In fact, it created a sustainable ecosystem where none existed, in order to sell its gizmos. So the right corollary for Blockbuster would be to invent new reasons for consumers to visit its stores. DVDs are Blockbuster's iPods, and once people don't need to fondle them any longer, I don't see what the company puts into its stores instead. Do you? Is that part of your remit?

3. Blockbuster is a habit, or routine, more than a choice. Nobody ever attached any meaning to it beyond perhaps, on the good side, an appreciation of its geographic convenience and, on the negatives, the potential to interact with surly or clueless employees (not to mention the reasonable probability that the title you wanted to rent is already checked out). Consumers used to stop by Blockbuster to "find something to watch" much like they'd pull up to a service station to "get some gas for the car." There's absolutely nothing wrong with that – like I said, I believe that such routines are immensely powerful – but it's certainly not entertaining.

Any stock analyst with a critical bone left in his or her body should be writing as much, but since we've been hearing this "entertainment brand" nonsense since, well, I was with the company in the mid 1990s, it should be old to someone other than me by now.

So any Blockbuster transformation would require a substantive change in the very premise of its business; it would have to be something far more meaningful than marketing, and a lot more inventive than anything we've ever heard before from the company. I have no idea what it might be, but I'm thinking things like giving away Blu-ray players to Blockbuster members, or building studios for UGC in every store.

The plans would have to originate in operations, and create a set of proprietary, value-add services only available in-store. Exclusive content from the studios, maybe events. Some reverse-logic distribution arrangement that was supported with actions that truly redefined why people needed to visit the stores. Big, structural, business-changing actions.

I suspect that making the brand more about entertainment is just not one of them. And this news should serve as a cautionary tale to other capable, well-intentioned, innovative marketers who might presume to fix client problems that they just not able to fix.

Epilogue: Stay Involved

OK, laughing yet?

I hope so. I say that if we're not having fun with this stuff, there's something wrong with us (or we've picked the wrong subject area to explore).

But I also wrote this book so it would find relevance to your work...not just immediately, but throughout the year...as proposals cross you desk, ideas pop into your mind, or when companies or subject areas appear in the news. *Perspective* is a precious commodity, and maybe this book can provide at least a small portion of it.

I can offer you more, too.

For starters, if you're not already a regular reader, I'd be thrilled if you'd subscribe to my blog, Dim Bulb. It's 100% free of ads, and my privacy policy is that I'll burn your information before sharing it with anybody, ever. You can RSS it, or sign-up for a weekly email blast that contains links to the most recent essays, quotes, and other relevant content. Just visit dimbulb.typepad. com

You can also get involved. More than half of the topics I write about are suggested by fellow dim bulbers. You don't have to subscribe, or even identify yourself in order to participate. Just send your ideas to dimbulb@baskinbrand.com

Please comment on my essays, too. Sometimes we get really good exchanges going. I promise to be respectful as long as you are; the best debates can arise if we totally disagree, so let's dive in.

You're also welcome to lift my ideas and riff on your own blog or site. Improve what I've said, or twist and shape it into something else. Let me know if you come up with something even better, so I can improve myself, too. When you see others posting comments that are distinctly un-dim-bulb-

ish, feel free to mention my blog, and/or throw out any of the ideas I've covered there.

Finally, I'd be thrilled if you'd post a review of this book at any site that sells it. Positive or negative. Your thoughts count.

My commitment is to keep doing my best to explore, analyze, and play with major marketing, branding, business, and cultural issues. I look forward to having that conversation with you.

Look for the 2011 edition of this book when most of our 2010 is history.

Primary Industry Categories
(by Essay #)

Advertising 63, 64, 66
Aerospace 31
Agriculture 35
Airlines 12, 23, 25, 28, 56
Automotive 13, 20, 26, 49, 55, 71, 86
Banking 10
Beverages 3, 18, 47, 50
Chemicals 38
Civic 1
Computers 15, 19. 39, 42
Cosmetics 14, 16
Energy 40
Fashion 46, 83
F & I 33, 48, 90
Food 24, 34, 72
Internet 29, 53, 58, 60, 62, 81, 85, 92
Mercenaries 2
Music 9
Newspapers 21, 43, 78
Pkg'd Goods 5, 44, 45
Pharma 8, 22
Non-Profit 41
Retailing 11, 32, 67, 79, 80, 82, 88, 89
Search 59, 74
Smartphones 6, 75, 84
Social media 7, 30, 52, 54, 57, 61, 65, 70, 87, 91
Software 4, 27. 36
Travel 37, 77
TV 17, 73
Video 51, 93

Name Index